Why Do You Need this New Edition?

If you're wondering why you should buy this new edition of *Sterling Stories*, here are 6 good reasons!

1. New stories from Sandra Cisneros and Kate Chopin have been added!

2. The book is now perforated so you can work on your studies right next to the story text.

3. A new Relationships theme has been added.

4. New Props, Foreshadowing, Irony, and Symbolism assignments have been added to the Journal to help you understand these literary concepts.

5. A new Literary Element assignment has been added to the Journal in order to help you understand all of the different concepts literature is made up of.

6. Updated MLA Works Cited format ensures you will have the most accurate information.

D0221860

Sterling Stories

12 Great Short Stories

SECOND EDITION

Yvonne Collioud Sisko

Middlesex County College

Illustrations by
John Seymour and Ted Sisko

PEARSON

Boston   Columbus   Indianapolis   New York   San Francisco   Upper Saddle River
Amsterdam   Cape Town   Dubai   London   Madrid   Milan   Munich   Paris   Montréal   Toronto
Delhi   Mexico City   São Paulo   Sydney   Hong Kong   Seoul   Singapore   Taipei   Tokyo

Senior Acquisitions Editor: Nancy Blaine
Development Editor: Jamie Fortner
Marketing Manager: Kurt Massey
Production Project Manager: Denise Philip
Production Manager: Maggie Brobeck
Project Coordination, Text Design, and

Electronic Page Makeup: Integra Software Services Pvt. Ltd.
Manager, Central Design: Jayne Conte
Cover Designer: Suzanne Duda
Cover Art: © nortivision/Shutterstock
Printer/Binder: Courier
Cover Printer: Courier

Library of Congress Cataloging-in-Publication Data
Sisko, Yvonne Collioud.
 Sterling stories : 12 great short stories/Yvonne Collioud Sisko; illustration by John Seymour and Ted Sisko.—2nd ed.
 p.   cm.
 Includes index.
 ISBN-13: 978-0-205-87412-5 (alk. paper)
 ISBN-10: 0-205-87412-6 (alk. paper)
 1. College readers.   2. English language—Rhetoric—Problems, exercises, etc.
3. Report writing—Problems, exercises, etc.   4. Short stories.   I. Title.
PE1417.S457 2014
808'.0427—dc23

                                                                2012036652

10 9 8 7 6 5 4 3 2 1—

ISBN 10:   0-205-87412-6
ISBN 13: 978-0-205-87412-5

To the children in my life—
To my grandson, Alex
To my children, Teddy and Laura
To my children-in-law, Jen and Dave
And to their cousins—
Jacob and Allison, Carrie and Reid and Missy
Renee, Scott, Abby and Owen
Lisa, Ashley, and Caitlin
Anthony and Christina
Robert, Kristyl, and Liahna

Contents

RIPE FIGS   A Sample Lesson   **1**

CHAPTER 1 Characters and Conflicts   **23**

CHAPTER 2 Setting and Props 59

Roch Carrier *The Hockey Sweater* 61

With political implications surrounding a central prop, Roch Carrier presents an interesting tale that will be appreciated by anyone who has rooted for a favorite team.

R. K. Narayan *Trail of the Green Blazer* 72

With an ironic turn of events, a thief is overcome by his own game and the things around him.

Mark Twain *Strong Temptations—Strategic Movements— The Innocents Beguiled* 84

Told with humor and irony, this is the classic tale of Tom Sawyer painting the fence.

CHAPTER 3 Plot and Foreshadowing   97

☞ Joseph Bruchac *Bone Girl*   98

There are morals and a classic example of foreshadowing in this informative ghost story.

☞ Max Brand *Wine on the Desert*   113

A story inside a story foreshadows the justice that is brutally served in this powerful story.

☞ Edgar Allan Poe *The Tell-Tale Heart*   129

Edgar Allan Poe walks the reader through the homicidal mind in this classic tale of maniacal obsession.

CHAPTER 4 Irony   143

❧ Catherine Lim   *Ah Bah's Money*   144

Told with a light touch, this story examines little Ah Bah and his family.

❧ Kate Chopin   *The Story of an Hour*   156

Kate Chopin turns marital assumptions upside down with her ironic twist.

❧ O. Henry   *Gifts of the Magi*   167

Love triumphs over all when gifts are well, if not wisely, given.

Intent and/or Tone
Contents

Here is a general listing of stories by themes, although most of these stories do not easily fit into one category or another. For instance, Twain's story of Tom Sawyer painting the fence can as easily be placed in *Irony*, *Triumph of the Spirit*, *Social Commentary*, or *Humor*.

TRIUMPH OF THE SPIRIT

These stories inspire and offer insight into the human condition.

HUMOR

These stories tickle the reader's funny bone.

IRONY

These stories come with unexpected twists.

SOCIAL COMMENTARY

These stories examine social and/or cultural issues.

RELATIONSHIPS

These stories focus on interpersonal relationships.

Foreword

With the successes of *American 24-Karat Gold, A World of Short Stories*, and *Looking at Literature*, we decided to create a collection of the most readable stories to introduce beginning students to literature and the relevant skills therein. *Sterling Stories* is that collection. We have taken the most succinct, most readable stories and have collected them here. Each story is still surrounded by the full complement of learning materials that are intended to maximize student learning while simultaneously maximizing teaching efficiency. In fact, among the now several thousand students who have field-tested these stories, we have seen dramatic increases in student performances in both reading and writing after studying these entries.

Many thanks go to each person whose interest, effort, and—especially—patience have supported me in this process. First, I heartily thank Lucille Alfieri, Betty Altruda, Jim Bernarducci, Debbie Brady, Santi Buscemi, Wilson Class, Gert Coleman, Jamie Daley, Sallie DelVecchio, Leah Ghiradella, Evelyn and Kristin Honey, Vernie Jarocki, Jim Keller, Angela Lugo, Ben Marshall, JoAnne McWilliams, Albert Nicolai, Jerry Olsen, Renee Price, Ellen Shur, Rich Strugala, Helena Swanicke, Shirley Wachtel and Dan Zimmerman, all dear friends and colleagues. I also thank Liz Oliu, Andre Gittens, library faculty at Middlesex who always seem to find the impossible for me. Then I must thank my cherished mentors—Drs. Dan O'Day, Bernie Weinstein, Bill Evans, Eileen Kennedy, Carla Lord, Carol Kouros-Shaffer, and Howard Didsbury—who ever inspire me. Special thanks go to the many students who have field-tested these materials and who continue to teach me what works and what does not work. And most special thanks go to Nancy Blaine, who brought this second edition to fruition, and to Jamie Fortner, who energetically assisted all along the way.

Special thanks go to my sisters, Michelle, Dodee, and Alice, who have often changed plans around my schedules. Super thanks go to my brother-in-law, John, and my son, Ted, whose illustrations light my books. My whole family thanks my son-in-law, Dave, for his computer expertise that has stopped many a technical tantrum on my part. And loving thanks always go to my son and my new daughter-in-law, Ted and Jen, my daughter and my son-in-law, Laura and Dave, and my fabulous grandson, Alex—they bring me joy everyday of my life. And, of course, special thanks go to my husband, George, who knows no longer to question what we're having for dinner, but rather where we are going for dinner.

This book is very dear to my heart. By choice, I have long taught our beginning students and I love teaching these students. I watch people not just become students, but I watch whole lives pull together as the academy becomes a viable path in their lives.

I truly hope you enjoy using this book as much as I have enjoyed developing it.

—Yvonne Collioud Sisko
Old Bridge, New Jersey

Preface

To the Student

It seems that human beings have always loved a good story. In fact, anthropologists tell us that story telling has been used to teach rules and ideas for millennia.

This book is filled with good stories, or narratives or narrations. Read these stories to gain knowledge about yourself, for a good story invariably offers us some information about ourselves. Most of all, read these stories to enjoy them. Stories have a way of taking us into new worlds, offering universals (feelings we all can understand).

However, the stories in this book are designed to do more than just expose you to each story itself. Each story is surrounded with exercises that will help you better understand it. Each story includes:

- **Vocabulary Exercises**—Vocabulary exercises help you define the words you need to know for the story, before you read it.
- **Questions**—Questions help guide you through the story.
- **Biography**—A biography of the story's author provides you with information about the author's style and other works.
- **Journal**—After reading, you can record and organize your thoughts about the story in a journal.
- **Follow-up Questions**—You can demonstrate what you've learned about the story in follow-up questions.
- **Discussion Questions**—These questions ask you to reach deeper and to react to the story.
- **Writing**—Writing ideas help to focus and guide your writing.

To better understand how this book works, turn to the Sample Lesson on page 1 and work your way through it. You'll find that you will be actively participating in this book, which will make understanding and appreciating the stories easier and more rewarding for you.

Welcome to *Sterling Stories*! Read this book, study it, and—most of all—enjoy it.

To the Teacher

The greatest assets of *Sterling Stories* are its participatory lessons and the many options these lessons offer you. Certainly, the literature is the core of this book, but the pedagogical materials that consistently surround every story require students to actively participate. Simultaneously, these materials offer you a choice of multiple, administratively efficient diagnostic and assessment tools. Each story is a self-contained lesson, and all the stories are consistently formatted, thereby offering students clear expectations and multiple options.

Sample Lesson

Sterling Stories starts out with an applied **Sample Lesson**. The Sample Lesson can be used in class, *or* it can be assigned as homework. Written in simple and accessible language, this introductory lesson walks students through the basic story format, using Kate Chopin's "Ripe Figs." This lesson, as all lessons, opens with Pre-reading Vocabulary—Context and Pre-reading Vocabulary—Structural Attack to help students define important words used in the story. Pre-reading Questions set purpose and an author biography supplies relevant background information.

After reading "Ripe Figs," students learn notation strategies that they can then apply to the subsequent readings. With the story completed, students move on to the Journal exercises, which are comprehensive and participatory studies of the story. The Sample Lesson explains the tasks in each Journal section, offers sample answers to get students started, and introduces relevant literary terminology.

With the Journal completed, students will have an active, working understanding of "Ripe Figs." They can then move on to three sets of Follow-up Questions. These questions consistently use multiple assessment formats: (1) ten multiple-choice questions objectively assessing comprehension; (2) five significant quotations subjectively assessing comprehension; and (3) two essay questions subjectively assessing comprehension. Then Discussion Questions ask students to reach deeper, to reflect upon, and to react to each story. Each story ends with Writing suggestions. In the Sample Lesson, students are introduced to pre-writing and outlining strategies. In subsequent stories, students will find multiple writing prompts.

I suggest that you work through the Sample Lesson in class, for it is here that you will find the dynamics and possibilities of this book encapsulated.

Chapter Structure

The stories in *Sterling Stories* are arranged into four topical chapters, based on and reinforcing the literary terminology the students have already encountered in the Sample Lesson. While all stories contain combinations of these terms and/or elements, each of the chapters focuses on a specific term(s) and/or element(s) by beginning with a restatement of the terms(s) and then by presenting the stories that have been specifically chosen to demonstrate the term(s) and/or element(s). Chapter 1 focuses on characters and conflicts, Chapter 2 focuses on setting and props, Chapter 3 focuses on plot and foreshadowing, and Chapter 4 focuses on irony.

Within each chapter, you have many options:

1. You can assign these chapters in any order.
2. You can also assign the stories within each chapter in any order. Generally, the stories within each chapter progress from more accessible to more difficult; but the strengths of each class vary, and what may seem more accessible for one group may be more difficult for another.
3. You can assign all the stories in a chapter or any number of stories you prefer.
4. You can use the alternative table of contents. Selecting from *Intent and/or Tone Contents* can make for interesting study.
5. All of these exercises are equally useable for individual assignments, for small group discussions, and/or for full class discussions.
6. You can ignore all these suggestions and assign any story at your discretion.

Story Structure

Each story in *Sterling Stories* is set amid carefully designed teaching materials, and because the format is consistent, you will be able to find these materials easily. These materials were discussed generally in the overview of the Sample Lesson above, but here we look at the materials more closely.

Pre-reading Materials

Each story selection begins with pre-reading materials. The pre-reading materials prepare students for reading each story while offering you insights into their vocabulary mastery and study habits.

    Pre-reading Vocabulary—Context presents words that are crucial to understanding the story. These words have been chosen to make the story accessible to students and may or may not be the most sophisticated words in the story.

    Pre-reading Vocabulary—Structural Attack offers structural analysis exercises. These words were chosen not for their sophistication, but because they help students apply structural analysis skills. Thus, before students start the story, they have defined at least 20 words in context and 10 to 30 more words in structural attack. The need for distracting glossed words and marginal definitions is thereby eliminated because students are well prepared by the pre-reading vocabulary to approach the story. Further, the Glossary at the end of the book supports students in this area and encourages referencing skills.

    Third, **Pre-reading Questions** offer food for thought as students enter the story. The author's **Biography** offers not only biographical background but also additional information about the author's other works.

Journal

After students have read and annotated the story, the **Journal** then draws them into active reflection and participation.

- *MLA Works Cited*—Students record the story in MLA Works Cited entry format, using the generic model provided (applying and reinforcing MLA format).
- *Main Character(s)*—Students separate, describe, and defend the character(s) they have selected as main character(s) (applying and reinforcing the separation of main ideas from details).
- *Supporting Characters*—Students separate, describe, and defend the characters they have selected as supporting characters (applying and reinforcing the separation of main ideas from supporting details).
- *Setting and Props*—Students describe and decide if they can change the setting (applying and reinforcing inference skills).
- *Sequence*—Students outline the story's events in order (applying and reinforcing sequencing and outlining skills).
- *Plot*—Students summarize the story's events in no more than two sentences (applying and reinforcing the separation of main ideas from supporting details, as well as summary skills).
- *Conflicts*—Students identify and explain the relevant conflicts (applying and reinforcing inference and judgment skills).
- *Significant Quotations*—Students explain the importance of quotations that are central to the story (applying and reinforcing inference skills).

- *Literary Elements*—Students reflect upon and explain the literary elements of each chapter as they are relevant to each story (applying and reinforcing judgment and synthesizing skills).
- *Foreshadowing, Irony, and Symbolism*—Students identify and explain these literary devices as each may apply to each story (applying and reinforcing sequencing, inference, and/or judgment skills).

The Journal is a comprehensive cognitive workout for students. In the Journal, students reflect on the story, sort out the details, and organize the story's components while applying and/or reinforcing their comprehension skills. You can collect any part or all of the Journal to check on student progress. The wealth of diagnostic information in the Journal will enable you to spot misunderstandings, illogical thinking, and so forth, that may compromise comprehension. Requiring a completed Journal for classroom participation also assures you of students who are prepared to discuss the story.

Follow-up Questions

The Journal is followed by three follow-up question formats. The Follow-up Questions are designed for assessment but can also be used for small group or class discussion. All of these questions are intended to measure comprehension; they purposely avoid literary controversy.

- **The section 10 Short Questions** offers ten multiple-choice questions.
- **The section 5 Significant Quotations** asks students to explain the importance of five quotations that are always central to the story.
- **The section 2 Comprehension Essay Questions** provides two essay prompts.

The Follow-up Questions offer you multiple, efficient assessment options. You may decide to use some questions for discussion or some for testing. If you are trying to establish standardization, the section of 10 Short Questions is applicable for measuring comprehension efficiently by psychometrically employing 10 questions with 3 choices each (only 6 are needed for accurate measurement).

Discussion Questions

Each story provides two thought-provoking questions. Unlike the Follow-up Questions, Discussion Questions encourage reflection, personal opinion, and/or literary debate. Again, you may choose to have students discuss these or to have students write these answers.

Writing Prompts

Each story concludes with options for **Writing**. Here, two prompts for personal writing are included. Then, under **Further Writing**, you will find prompts for more challenging, research-oriented writing. These prompts may be literary (compare and contrast this story with another in this book, with another by this author, with one by another author, and so forth) or topical research suggestions.

Some Final Notes

The materials in *Sterling Stories*—the context and structural vocabulary exercises, the journal format, the three assessment options, the discussion questions, as well as the many writing prompts—have been extensively field-tested by more than two thousand students. These field tests have taken place in one of the most culturally diverse counties in America—Middlesex County, New Jersey. Three major results have occurred. First, student competencies in both reading and writing have dramatically increased. Second, these stories have also come to serve as a basis for acculturation discussions with ESL and/or international students. Third, the pedagogical materials have been streamlined to maximize learning efficacy and to maximize administrative efficiency simultaneously.

To further assist you, I have added a section in the appendix on "How *I* Use This Book." This has been written in response to the many enthusiastic questions I received on this book, and I hope this will be of use to you.

It should also be noted that, although copyright restrictions apply, we have elided offensive words wherever feasible.

Last, but certainly not least, we must address the stories themselves. The richness of the literature speaks for itself, and the stories have been most carefully chosen to combine the best of writers with the most readable of stories. This collection sets out to expand the literary lexicon of today's entering students.

I sincerely hope you and your students enjoy reading these stories as much as I have enjoyed working with them.

—Yvonne Collioud Sisko
Old Bridge, New Jersey

A SAMPLE LESSON

Ripe Figs

by

Kate Chopin

The best way to learn how to use something is to do just that—to use it. This Sample Lesson presents a very short work, "Ripe Figs" by Kate Chopin, to demonstrate how this book works. This Sample Lesson presents all the materials that surround each story. Generally, each reading starts with pre-reading activities that are designed to make your reading easier, and ends with a journal, follow-up questions, discussion questions, and writing assignments that are designed to improve your understanding. This Sample Lesson also introduces the elements of a narrative—elements that you will be using throughout this book.

Let's begin.

1

Ripe Figs

KATE CHOPIN

PRE-READING VOCABULARY
CONTEXT

Use context clues to define these words before reading. Use a dictionary as needed.

The words that are critical for your understanding of the reading are presented at the beginning of each reading. These are not necessarily the most difficult words. Rather, they are words that you will need to know to understand the reading more easily.

The **Pre-reading Vocabulary—Context** exercises present words in sentences. You should try to define each word by using the **context clues** in the sentence. Note that the first eight words have been defined as examples for you. Look at sentence 1. The word here is "fig," and the clues let you know that this is something "small" and "purple" that grows "on a tree" and is "delicious." Since "delicious" implies it is something to eat and since fruit grows on a tree, we can define a "fig" as "a small, purple fruit that grows on a tree." Using this same strategy, check the meanings of the next seven words. Then use the clues and define the remaining words.

1. The small, purple *figs* grow on a tree and are delicious. *Fig* means
   <u>a small, purple fruit that grows on a tree.</u>

2. Some may say "mom" or "mama" for "mother," while the French may say *mère* or *maman*. *Mére* or *maman* means
   <u>a name for "mother."</u>

3. The campers rowed their boat slowly through the reeds along the side of the *bayou*. *Bayou* means <u>a slow-moving body of water.</u>

4. The children licked the long *sugar cane* they found in the field. *Sugar cane* means <u>a stick-like food.</u>

5. The elderly person's fingers seemed to cross each other in *gnarled* knots from old age and arthritis. *Gnarled* means
   <u>knotted and crisscrossed.</u>

6. Ted is so *patient*; he doesn't mind if Laura takes two hours to do her hair. *Patient* means <u>willing to wait.</u>

7. There is a stone *statue* of a little boy in the middle of the garden. *Statue* means <u>a carved or sculpted figure.</u>

8. The tiny *humming-bird's* wings moved so quickly that you could not see them. *Humming-bird* means <u>a small bird with rapidly moving wings.</u>

9. Dave was *disconsolate* after he lost the championship game. *Disconsolate* means _____.

10. Kings and queens usually walk in a very dignified and *stately* manner. *Stately* means _____.

11. Furniture is often first covered in a simple *muslin* under the fine fabric to protect the fabric. *Muslin* means _____.

12. The haze of color often drawn around a saint's head is called a halo or *aureole*. *Aureole* means _____.

13. In spite of all the upset and confusion, Alex stayed cool and *placid*. *Placid* means _____.

14. The bride's dishes are fine *porcelain* decorated with tiny flowers and trimmed in gold. *Porcelain* means _____.

15. I will go to see my aunt, *Tante* Lena, to celebrate her birthday. *Tante* means _____.

16. I love the large yellow *chrysanthemums* that bloom in a fall garden. *Chrysanthemum* means _____.

PRE-READING VOCABULARY
STRUCTURAL ATTACK

Define these words by solving the parts. Use the Glossary or a dictionary as needed.

The **Pre-reading Vocabulary—Structural Attack** exercises present words that you know but that may look strange or have altered meanings because of added parts. Here you will want to look for and define the **root**, or core, word. Then look for and define the **prefix**, or part added to the front of the word. Finally, look for and define the **suffix**, or part added to the end of the word.

Prefixes (added to the front) and suffixes (added to the end) are called **affixes**. By defining the root and the affixes, you should be able to define each of these words with little trouble. For instance, look at the first vocabulary word. The very simple word "ripe" has two suffixes (-en, -ing) that can be added to it, which change the word's meaning from "ready" or "mature" to "getting ready" or "maturing." Or words may combine to become a **compound word**. Look at the fourth word. "Summer" and "time" combine to mean "warm time of the year."

Using these same strategies, take each word apart, and define it by using the roots and affixes. The next two words are defined for you also. Try the last three on your own. See the Glossary (page 185) for affix definitions.

1. ripening   *becoming ripe or mature*
2. la Madone   *mother or Holy Mother*
3. restless   *active; cannot rest*
4. summertime
5. godmother
6. plumpest

PRE-READING QUESTIONS

Try answering these questions as you read.

Before reading, it is always helpful to start with a purpose. Use the reading's title and any other relevant information to set up questions to answer while you are reading. Answering these questions will make your reading easier and more efficient, so that you do not have to read and reread to understand the narrative.

Each reading starts with **Pre-reading Questions** to set your purpose. Keep these questions in mind as you read.

Who are the main characters? Supporting characters?

What does Babette want?

What does Maman want?

What does the title mean?

Ripe Figs

Kate Chopin

Before each narrative, a brief **biography** provides some information about the author. In addition to learning about the author's life, you may also pick up information that will help you in reading the narrative. The biography may also list other works by the author, in case you would like to read more by that author.

Read Kate Chopin's biography. It tells you, among other things, that she writes about the people she met in Louisiana and that she likes to use "symbols and images from nature." Both of these pieces of information will come in handy as you read "Ripe Figs."

Kate O'Flaherty Chopin was born in St. Louis in 1851 to an affluent family. Although her father died when she was young, her widowed mother gave young Kate a taste of independence. In 1870 Kate married Oscar Chopin and moved to New Orleans and then Natchitoches Parish. Here she met the Creoles, Acadians, and African Americans she would later write about. Oscar died in 1882, and by 1884 she sold the plantation, gathered her five children, and returned home to St. Louis, where she began to write for popular women's magazines. Influenced noticeably by Guy de Maupassant's sense of irony and Henrik Ibsen's social comment, Chopin wrote stories, often touched with rich symbols and images from nature, that question societal assumptions and dictates. *The Awakening* remains her master work, although short stories offer Chopin at her most terse. Chopin died in 1904.

Now it is time to turn to the reading. As you read, keep the following suggestions in mind. Don't just let your eyes go over words. Instead, *get involved—get out a pen or pencil and highlighters, and use them!*

1. First, *circle the name of each character*, or highlight each in a different color. The first step in understanding a narrative is knowing *whom* it is about.
2. Second, underline or highlight in yet another color all the hints that let you know *where and when* the narrative takes place. The second step in understanding a narrative is knowing *where and when* it takes place.
3. Third, *number each event* in the narrative as it occurs. Number these events in the margin or right in the text. The third step in understanding a narrative is knowing *what* is happening.
4. Fourth, *make notes*—ideas, questions to be answered later, and so on—in the margin. These are ideas you can return to later, and they may help you understand the *how* and/or *why* of the narrative.
5. Fifth, but certainly not least, always *reread the title*. The title often gives you information that is helpful in understanding the narrative.

Maman-Nainaine said that when the figs were ripe Babette might go to visit her cousins down on the Bayou-Lafourche where the sugar cane grows. Not that the ripening of figs had the least thing to do with it, but that is the way Maman-Nainaine was.

2   It seemed to Babette a very long time to wait; for the leaves upon the trees were tender yet, and the figs were like little hard, green marbles.

3   But warm rains came along and plenty of strong sunshine, and though Maman-Nainaine was as patient as the statue of la Madone, and Babette as restless as a humming-bird, the first thing they both knew it was hot summertime. Every day Babette danced out to where the fig-trees were in a long line against the fence. She walked slowly beneath them, carefully peering between the gnarled, spreading branches. But each time she came away disconsolate again. What she saw there finally was something that made her sing and dance the whole day long.

4   When Maman-Nainaine sat down in her stately way to breakfast, the following morning, her muslin cap standing like an aureole around her white, placid face, Babette approached. She bore a dainty porcelain platter, which she set down before her godmother. It contained a dozen purple figs, fringed around with their rich, green leaves.

5   "Ah," said Maman-Nainaine arching her eyebrows, "how early the figs have ripened this year!"

6   "Oh," said Babette. "I think they have ripened very late."

7   "Babette," continued Maman-Nainaine, as she peeled the very plumpest figs with her pointed silver fruit-knife, "you will carry my love to them all down on Bayou-Lafourche. And tell your Tante Frosine I shall look for her at Toussaint—when the chrysanthemums are in bloom."

Now turn to the marked copy of "Ripe Figs" in Figure 1. The first half has already been noted for you. Take out your pen, pencil, and/or highlighters, and using the strategies listed above, complete the notes on "Ripe Figs." Note how effective the notations in Figure 1 are. It's important to know that Chopin uses nature to reflect life, so this is underlined in the biography. The title is "Ripe Figs," so figs (which are a delicate fruit) must somehow relate to the story. Babette and Maman-Nainaine are in the center of the story, and the cousins and Tante Frosine are also involved. Hints like "figs" and "Bayou," as well as information in the biography, all indicate that this story is probably taking place in the South, in Louisiana. The events are numbered in sequence: (1) Babette wants to go visiting, but Maman says not yet; (2) Babette must wait for the figs to ripen; (3) the figs ripen, and Babette now can go; and (4) Maman will go in the fall. Now it is easier to see that two things are ripening or maturing here: Babette and the figs. Thus, the ripening figs reflect Babette's maturing. When the figs are ripe, she is also ripe—or mature enough—to go visiting. By using the information from the biography and title and combining this information with the story's characters, setting, and events, you can see that as the figs ripen, Babette grows older and becomes ready to travel. Add your own notes in paragraphs 4 through 7.

FIGURE 1
Marked Copy of "Ripe Figs"

Ripe Figs

KATE CHOPIN

Kate O'Flaherty Chopin was born in St. Louis in 1851 to an affluent family. Although her father died when she was young, her widowed mother gave young Kate a taste of independence. In 1870 Kate married Oscar Chopin and moved to New Orleans and then Natchitoches Parish. Here she met the Creoles, Acadians, and African Americans she would later write about. However, Oscar died in 1882, and by 1884 she sold the plantation, gathered her five children, and returned home to St. Louis, where she began to write for popular women's magazines. Influenced noticeably by Guy de Maupassant's sense of irony and Henrik Ibsen's social comment, Chopin wrote stories, often touched with rich symbols and <u>images from nature,</u> that question societal assumptions and dictates. *The Awakening* remains her master work, although short stories offer Chopin at her most terse. Chopin died in 1904.

Maman-Nainaine said that when the figs were ripe Babette might go to visit her cousins down on the <u>Bayou-Lafourche</u> where the <u>sugar cane grows</u>. Not that the ripening of figs had the least thing to do with it, but that is the way Maman-Nainaine was.

> 1. CAN VISIT WHEN FIGS RIPEN

2 It seemed to Babette a very long time to wait; for the leaves upon the trees were tender yet, and the figs were like little hard, green marbles.

3 But <u>warm rains</u> came along and plenty of <u>strong sunshine</u>, and though Maman-Nainaine was as patient as the statue of la Madone, and Babette as restless as a humming-bird, the first thing they both knew it was <u>hot summertime</u>. Every day Babette danced out to where the fig-trees were in a long line against the fence. She walked slowly beneath them, carefully peering between the gnarled, spreading branches. But each time she came away disconsolate again. What she saw there finally was something that made her sing and dance the whole day long.

> 2. WAIT FOR FIGS TO GROW

4 When Maman-Nainaine sat down in her stately way to breakfast, the following morning, her muslin cap standing like an aureole around her white, placid face, Babette approached. She bore a dainty porcelain platter, which she set down before her godmother. It contained a dozen purple figs, fringed around with their rich, green leaves.

5 "Ah," said Maman-Nainaine arching her eyebrows, "how early the figs have ripened this year!"

6 "Oh," said Babette. "I think they have ripened very late."

7 "Babette," continued Maman-Nainaine, as she peeled the very plumpest figs with her pointed silver fruit-knife, "you will carry my love to them all down on Bayou-Lafourche. And tell your Tante Frosine I shall look for her at Toussaint—when the chrysanthemums are in bloom."

Ripe Figs

JOURNAL

> Once you have finished reading and making your notes on the reading, the **Journal** allows you to record and organize all the relevant information. Here you will be able to record, to organize, to reflect upon, and to make sense out of all the details that can make a reading challenging.

1. MLA Works Cited   *Using this model, record your reading here.*

Author's Last Name, First Name. "Title of the Story." *Title of the Book.*

2nd ed. Ed. First Name Last Name. City: Publisher, year. Page number(s) of

this story. Print.

> Whenever you refer to or use anyone else's words or ideas, you must give that person credit. Failing to give credit is called **plagiarism.** Plagiarism can result in failing an assignment, failing a course, and even being removed from school.
>
>   To give credit appropriately, it is helpful to learn the format used to credit works of literature and, in this sample, short stories are literature. This format has been created by the MLA, which is short for Modern Language Association. The **MLA Works Cited entry** you use here is the same form you will be using in your other English classes.
>
>   The MLA entry is really a very simple form. All you have to do is follow the model given. Note that, unlike paragraphs, the first line starts at the left margin and each line *after* that is indented. Also note that, generally, titles of major works and/or collections are italicized, while titles of shorter works and/or entries within a collection are put in quotation marks. Try doing this on your own. When you finish, your MLA Works Cited entry should look like the following:

Chopin, Kate. "Ripe Figs." *Sterling Stories.* 2nd ed. Ed. Yvonne Sisko.

New York: Pearson Longman, 2014, 7. Print.

2. Main Character(s)

> **Characters** are the creatures that create, move, or experience the actions of a narrative. We normally think of characters as alive, animated beings, such as humans or animals, who can participate in the action, although some characters will surprise you. A character may also be called an **actor, player, person, personage,** or **persona.**
>
>   Characters fall into two categories: main characters and supporting characters. Generally, a **main character** is central to the action. A **supporting character** may

encourage the action and is usually not present as much, nor as central to the action, as the main character. Sometimes it is difficult to decide if a character is main or supporting. For instance, in a murder mystery, the victim may appear at the beginning or not at all, but the entire narrative is about solving her or his murder. Is the victim a main character because the entire narrative is all about her or him, or is s/he a supporting character because s/he is simply not around much? Both answers may be correct. In literature there are not always so much right or wrong answers as there are explanations, analyses, and debates. The correctness of your answers may depend on how well you explain your choices.

Characters may also be considered protagonists or antagonists. "Pro" means "for," and the **protagonist** is the hero or heroine, the character we **empathize** with or share feelings with, the character we root for. "Anti" means "against," and the **antagonist** is the villain, the enemy of the protagonist, the character we do not like, the character we root against. In "Ripe Figs," our sympathies are with Babette and her longing for adventure; she is the protagonist. Maman, who sets limits on Babette, is the antagonist. Here, these two characters are members of a seemingly close family and love each other, but in other narratives the protagonist and antagonist may not be such close relatives and/or friends.

The author speaks to us through her or his characters. When an author writes using "I" or "we," this is called a **first-person narrative**. The first person makes a story very immediate. The character who tells the story is called the **narrator**. If the author addresses the reader directly using "you," this narrative technique is called a **second-person narrative**. Second person is not used often today. Finally, if the author uses "he," "she," "it," or "they" to tell the narrative, this narrative technique is called a **third-person narrative**. This is the most common narrative form, with the author seeming to be more of an observer and less of a participant in the story. In "Ripe Figs," both Babette and Maman are observed as "she." The story is thus told in the third person; the author is the narrator who observes but does not enter the narrative.

With these understandings, turn to the **Main Character(s)** and **Supporting Characters** entries in the Journal. Note that we have already filled in Babette, briefly describing her and noting her important place in the story. Who else should be here? Add an entry in which you describe and defend Maman as a main character.

Note: When discussing literature, always use the **present tense**. Although a narrative may have been written a thousand years ago, each time a narrative is read the characters and actions come to life and are alive right now, so keep your discussions of the characters and events in the present tense.

Describe each main character, and explain why you think each is a main character.

> Babette is a young girl who lives with her godmother and wants to go visit her cousins. She is a main character because the story is about her wants and her godmother's rules.

3. Supporting Characters

Now fill in the **Supporting Characters** entry. This has been started for you. Certainly, the cousins support the action because they are the reason Babette wants to travel. Who else should be here? Add an entry in which you describe and defend Tante Frosine as a supporting character. Remember from your context studies that "tante" means "aunt," so Tante Frosine is probably the cousins' mother.

Describe each supporting character, and explain why you think each is a supporting character.

> Babette's cousins are supporting characters. Although we never see them, they are the reason for the story's conflict.

4. Setting and Props

Setting is a catch all term that describes the **time, place,** and **surroundings** of a narrative. In a short story, the setting is usually, although not always, limited. The story usually takes place in a shorter amount of time than in a longer work, and fewer places are involved. In a novel, there may be more time and more places.

Props go along with the setting. Props (short for "properties") are the inanimate objects in a narrative. Props sometimes take on the qualities of characters.

Now turn to the **Setting** entry. You already have a head start because the place, Louisiana, is described. But you still have several things to do. First, you need to add when the story takes place. Check the biography for when Chopin lived, and remember that traveling seems to be a very big accomplishment in this story, unlike it is in today's world of easy car transportation. Second, think about props and mention the figs, which are certainly part of this story. Here, the place has been done for you. Now, add your descriptions of the time and any relevant props.

Describe the setting(s) and any relevant prop(s).

> This must be set in the South because figs are a delicate fruit, because the French words sound like words spoken in Louisiana, and because the biography says that Chopin wrote about the South.

5. Sequence

A narrative is based around a simple skeleton of events called a **plot**. Around this basic plot, a logical order of events or **sequence** occurs that builds tension or, in mysteries, suspense. In narratives we call all the events in the sequence a **story line**. The plot is the bare framework, while the sequence supplies the details that make each narrative unique.

Have you ever gone to the movies and watched the end credits roll while you were still waiting for the movie to get going? You looked at the person sitting next to you, felt cheated, and asked, "What happened?" What happened is that, somewhere along the line, the storyteller failed.

In a well-written narrative, one event logically leads to another, and then to another, and so on, so that each word and action counts and builds tension that carries your interest. The tension peaks at the **climax** and then resolves in the **dénouement**. When any of these pieces are missing, poorly developed, or unbelievable, we are disappointed. (Movie sequels, in fact, purposely stop at the climax and before the dénouement so that we will return for the next episode.) A very simple story line appears in Figure 2.

FIGURE 2
Simple Story Line

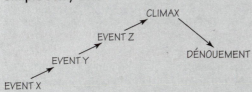

Record information about sequence and plot in the Journal. In the **Sequence** entry, you are asked to outline all the events in order. The outline is started for you, with Babette's desire to go visiting and Maman's restriction. Now look at your numbered notes on the story, and complete the outline. Add as many events as you feel are necessary.

Outline the events of the story in order.

I. Babette wants to go visiting, but Maman-Nainaine says she must wait for the figs to ripen.

II.

III.

IV.

6. Plot

Next, in the **Plot** entry, summarize all these events into one sentence. Summarizing makes you look back over the reading and reflect on what you have read. Remember, this is the bare framework of the narrative, so keep it short.

Tell the story in no more than one sentence.

7. Conflicts

Conflicts are the disagreements between the characters. Conflicts build the tension in a narrative. Many types of conflicts are possible. The conflict may be **human versus human**, as when a character(s) is pitted against another character(s). The conflict may be **human versus society**, as when a character(s) struggles against a group, community, or social structure. The conflict may be **human versus technology**, as when a character(s) vies with the tools of science or machines of society. The conflict may be **human versus nature,** as when a character(s) battles with the forces of nature. The conflict may be **human versus the supernatural**, as when a character(s) vies with God or gods or demons. Finally, the conflict may be **human versus herself/himself**, as when a character wrestles with her or his own internal and self-defeating **flaw**. More often than not, a story will contain a combination of these conflicts.

Let's now turn to the **Conflicts** entry. Human versus human, in Babette's struggle with Maman's restriction, is already noted. What other types of conflicts are present in the story? How about human versus nature in Babette's wanting the figs to mature rapidly, and human versus herself in Babette's impatience? Add these and explain them in your Journal entry.

Identify and explain all the conflicts involved here.

Human versus human applies to Babette wanting to go and Maman-Nainaine stopping her.

8. Significant Quotations

By now, you already understand the narrative well. You have identified the pieces and pulled them together. Now you need to reflect on the narrative. In this section, you will find quotations from key parts of the narrative. By explaining why each quotation is important to the reading, you can deepen your understanding.

First, look up the quotation in the reading text. Underline it and note what is important about this moment in the reading. Then, record the importance of this moment. Tell who is speaking and why this quotation is important to the action in the reading. The first one has been done for you. Now, complete the rest. Record the page number for practice with **MLA parenthetical citation.**

Explain the importance of each of these quotations. Record the page number in the parentheses.

a. "Maman-Nainaine said that when the figs were ripe Babette might go to visit her cousins down on the Bayou-Lafourche where the sugar cane grows" (7).

   This quotation sets the tension in the story between Babette and Maman-Nainaine and between Babette and nature. Babette wants to visit her cousins, but she must wait until the figs—and she—are ripe or mature enough to go.

b. "Every day Babette danced out to where the fig-trees were in a long line against the fence" ( ).

c. "What she saw there finally was something that made her sing and dance the whole day long" ( ).

d. "'Ah,' said Maman-Nainaine arching her eyebrows, 'how early the figs have ripened this year!'" (   ).

e. "'And tell your Tante Frosine I shall look for her at Toussaint—when the chrysanthemums are in bloom'" (   ).

9. Literary Elements

By now, you have become familiar with identifying characters, conflicts, settings, props, sequences, plots, and so forth. These terms or ideas, along with others you will meet, are called **literary elements**. You will see that the chapters in this book stress specific elements. Here you are asked to decide why each story is placed in the chapter in which it appears.

For instance, let's say that "Ripe Figs" had been placed in the *Characters and Conflicts* chapter. "Ripe Figs" not only has characters and conflicts, but certainly also has a setting and important props, and it certainly has events leading up to a climax. Yet in looking over the whole story, we can see that this story is largely a character study focused on impatient Babette and the conflicts her impatience entails. Thus, here you will want to focus on why characters and conflicts are so important in this story. Likewise, for every other story, you will focus on the chapter's literary element(s) and explain why the element(s) is (are) important to the story. Sometimes you may even disagree with the placement and, if you disagree, explain why you disagree and where else you would place the story. The important thing is that you explain the story in terms of the given element(s). Now, explain why characters and conflicts are so important in "Ripe Figs." Then explain any other chapter(s) in which you feel "Ripe Figs" might also fit.

Look at this chapter's title [here, we are using Characters and Conflicts] and explain why you think this story is placed in this chapter. Explain in which other chapter(s) you might place this story, as relevant to the literary element(s) of that chapter.

10. Foreshadowing, Irony, and/or Symbolism

Other elements that may enhance a narrative are foreshadowing, irony, and/or symbolism.

Foreshadowing is a technique some authors use to help explain or predict events to come. The author may sprinkle information or hints throughout the narrative to help predict actions that are yet to happen.

Irony is found in the difference between what *is* and what *should be.* Irony may be bitter—you work and work and work, and someone new, who has done nothing, arrives at your job and gets the promotion you deserve. Irony may be humorous—you wake up late and race around knowing you will be late for class, only to get to school and find out that your class has been canceled. Irony may even be providential—you sleep in and miss your bus, only to find out that the bus has been in an accident and you are still safe at home. Think of ironies as <u>unexpected twists</u> in time, places, or events.

Symbols are objects or characters that represent something beyond their face value. For instance, an American flag is really nothing more than pieces of cloth sewn together, but the American flag represents the pride and glory and industry of America. By looking beyond the surface, you will find many examples of symbolism in literature.

In **Foreshadowing, Irony, and/or Symbolism**, you will want to discuss one of these elements. Here, let's focus on the symbols in this story, and there are several. First and foremost, the figs represent maturity and reflect Babette's growth. Second, the **seasons** are relevant here. Summer is youthful Babette's time, while fall is the older Maman's and Tante Frosine's time. In literature, spring may represent birth or rebirth or youth; summer may represent youth or the full blossom of life; fall may represent middle age; and winter may represent the later years. Here Chopin gives us clues to the characters' ages by using the seasons. The chrysanthemums (flowers that bloom in the fall) represent the time for Babette's elders.

Although foreshadowing and irony are not particularly relevant to this story, be aware that Kate Chopin is known for her ironic twists. "The Story of an Hour" (page 159) takes a wonderfully unexpected turn. And, of course, here the ripening figs foreshadow Babette's growth.

Explain examples of foreshadowing, irony, and/or symbolism in this story.

Follow-up Questions
10 SHORT QUESTIONS

Follow-up questions are designed to measure your comprehension of each reading. In the first set of questions, **10 Short Questions**, you will see ten multiple-choice entries aimed at measuring your comprehension.

Notice that you are instructed to "select the <u>best</u> answer." In some readings, more than one answer will be correct; it is your job to choose the <u>best</u> answer. The first five have been done for you here.

The answer to question 1 is "a" because Babette is the younger of the two. We know this because Babette's actions and the information from the story—Maman means "mother" and Maman is Babette's godmother—imply that Babette is younger and Maman is older. The answer to question 2 is "b" for the same reasons listed in the answer to question 1. The answer to question 3 is "c" because we are clearly told that Maman is the godmother. The cousins are in Babette's age group and are whom she wants to visit; there is no mention of a sister in the story. The answer to question 4 is "a," because, as the story implies, figs need a warm summer and rain to grow; neither "cold" nor "desert" fit the story's setting. The answer to question 5 is "c," because we are clearly told about Babette's "restlessness" as opposed to Maman's "patience."

Now complete questions 6 through 10 on your own. The correct answers appear on page 21.

What is the <u>best</u> answer for each?

_a_ 1. Babette is
   a. younger than Maman.
   b. older than Maman.
   c. the same age as Maman.

_b_ 2. Maman-Nainaine is
   a. younger than Babette.
   b. older than Babette.
   c. the same age as Babette.

_c_ 3. Maman-Nainaine is Babette's
   a. sister.
   b. cousin.
   c. godmother.

_a_ 4. "Ripe Figs" is probably set in
   a. a warm climate.
   b. a cold climate.
   c. a desert climate.

_c_ 5. Babette
   a. does not wait for the figs.
   b. waits calmly for the figs.
   c. waits impatiently for the figs.

____ 6. Maman
   a. does not wait for the figs.
   b. waits calmly for the figs.
   c. waits impatiently for the figs.

_____ 7. The figs symbolize
    a. Maman's maturing.
    b. Babette's maturing.
    c. Babette's cousins'
       maturing.

_____ 8. We can infer that Maman is
    relatively
    a. poor.
    b. middle class.
    c. well off.

_____ 9. We can infer that the cousins
    live
    a. nearby.
    b. a distance away.
    c. very, very far away.

_____ 10. The chrysanthemums tell us
    that Maman is
    a. very young.
    b. very old.
    c. in her middle years.

5 SIGNIFICANT QUOTATIONS

Approach these **5 Significant Quotations** by reflecting on the reading. The quotations are important and central to the reading. Remember that you are demonstrating how well you have understood the reading, so explain why each quotation is important as completely as you can.

The first quotation here has already been done for you. Now, explain the significance of the remaining four. The answers are on page 21.

What is the importance of each of these quotations?

1. "Maman-Nainaine said that when the figs were ripe Babette might go to visit her cousins down on the Bayou-Lafourche where the sugar cane grows."

   This sentence sets the tension in the story between Babette and Maman-Nainaine and between Babette and nature. Babette wants to visit her cousins, but she must wait until the figs—and she—are ripe or mature enough.

2. "It seemed to Babette a very long time to wait; [...]."

3. "But warm rains came along and plenty of strong sunshine, and though Maman-Nainaine was as patient as the statue of la Madone, and Babette as restless as a humming-bird, the first thing they both knew it was hot summertime."

4. "It [the platter] contained a dozen purple figs, fringed around with their rich, green leaves."

5. "'Babette,' continued Maman-Nainaine, as she peeled the very plumpest figs with her pointed silver fruit-knife, 'you will carry my love to them all down on Bayou-LaFourche.'"

2 Comprehension Essay Questions

The **2 Comprehension Essay Questions** offer opportunities for extended essays. Your teacher may assign one or both for individual assignment or for group discussion. Gather your thoughts and respond, demonstrating what you have learned from the reading. Note that none of these questions asks how well you liked the reading or even if you liked it at all. The intention here is very simply to find out what you have understood in the reading.

Note that the directions ask you to "use specific details and information from the story." This does not mean that you have to memorize the reading, but it does mean that you should know the characters and events in the reading. Look at question 1. It asks you to explain the title, so for this essay question, you will want to review the story's events and the relevance of the figs. Now look at question 2. It asks you to focus on the ages involved in the story, and for this you will want to discuss the ages of Babette and her cousins as opposed to those of Maman and Tante Frosine, remembering the references to summer and fall in the story.

Use specific details and information from the story to answer these questions as completely as possible.

1. How does the title relate to the story? Explain the significance of the title using specific details and information from the story.

2. What is the relevance of age in this story? Use specific details and information from the story to support your explanation.

Discussion Questions

Now that you have read and studied the narrative, **Discussion Questions** are two questions that are always focused on the narrative and that are designed to help you think about the narrative. Here, you may be asked to share your opinions or reactions to elements in the narrative. Notice that you are instructed to "be prepared to discuss these questions in class." Although your teacher may ask you to discuss these questions as a class or to write the answers independently, your thoughtful answers should reflect what you have learned about the reading. The first one has been started for you.

Here, you need to reflect on the story and on your own youth. You need to identify and explain what characteristics you think Babette possesses that are youthful. Of course, when one thinks of youth, one thinks of energy, and you might want to discuss Babette's activities that require lots of energy, such as being physically busy and active, surrounding oneself with busy friends, and so forth. Related to energy, one thinks of impatience when one thinks of youth, and you may want to discuss Babette's impatience with the figs and Maman and traveling. Finally, the curiosity to explore or, in this case, to travel may also be a sign of youth, and you may want to discuss Babette's desire to travel. Think if there is anything else you might want to add to question 1.

Then, reflect on the story and on your own observations of mature people. Complete question 2 on your own.

Be prepared to discuss these questions in class.

1. What characteristics mark Babette's youth?

> One characteristic of youth is having lots of energy. Babette is continually in motion, expending a great deal of physical energy. She is also looking forward to visiting with her cousins, and visiting also requires a great deal of energy. With all this energy, another characteristic of youth is impatience. Babette is impatient with Maman, wanting to speed the ripening of the figs to suit Maman's rules. Babette is also impatient with the figs themselves, as she spends much time and energy checking and wishing them into ripening. And Babette is impatient to travel. Curiosity and inquisitiveness are often associated with the young, and Babette has both the energy and the curiosity to look forward to this trip.

2. What characteristics mark Maman's maturity?

WRITING

Each narrative ends with a final section of **Writing** prompts. The first two prompts offer suggestions for personal writing. The prompts under **Further Writing** are designed with research in mind. These may suggest comparing and contrasting the reading with other readings in this book or with other narratives the author or another author has written, or they may suggest other research topics. Your teacher will guide you through the writing process.

At this point, a few words about the writing process are in order. Writing does not start with a pen or pencil; it starts with ideas. Before you start writing, jot down ideas, and then organize them. Here are two **pre-writing strategies** to get the ideas flowing:

1. On a clean sheet of paper, write one key word based on the topic you plan to write about. Now look at the key word, and start listing every word that this key word brings to mind. Avoid sentences or even phrases, as they take longer to write and can break your train of thought. Just write words—lots

of words, the more the merrier. When you run out of words, look back at the key word, and write more words. When you finish, you will have a whole list of ideas to start thinking about for your essay. This process is called **free associating** or **brainstorming.**

2. On a clean sheet of paper, draw a circle. Inside that circle, write one key word about the topic on which you plan to write. Now look at the key word, and start tagging other, related words onto the circle. Then tag words onto the tag words, and so on. When you get stuck, look back at the key word, and add more words. When you finish, you will have groups of words—ideas—to start thinking about for your essay. This process is called **grouping, networking,** or **clustering.**

Once you have the ideas—and you should have plenty from either of these pre-writing strategies—the next step is to organize them into an **outline.** Do not worry about Roman numerals at this stage. Rather, develop logical groupings of these ideas into a working outline. You may find that there are words/ideas in your pre-write that you do not want to use. Cross these out. You may also find ideas in your outline that are out of place. Number and renumber the groups to make them work for you. (Your instructor may want you to formalize your outline later, but at this point the important thing is to find an organization that works for you.)

Look at the first writing prompt below. It asks you, first, to discuss one specific maturing process you have experienced and, second, to relate this process to a reflective image, much like the figs in our story. In Figure 3 both a cluster and an outline on the topic "Getting a License" are demonstrated, but you may want to try "Learning to Ride a Bike" or "Graduating from High School" or any other maturing process you prefer.

FIGURE 3
Sample Cluster and Outline

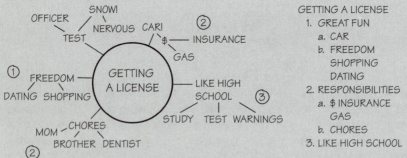

To prepare the pre-writing cluster and outline shown in Figure 3, we first tagged ideas onto "License" and then tagged ideas onto ideas. Second, we looked for a logical order and numbered and renumbered the cluster. Third, we transferred these numbers into the informal, working outline. Finally, we looked back over what we had and decided that getting a license was like attending high school, because of all the preparation and responsibility involved in getting a license. With these ideas initiated and organized, we are now ready to write an intelligent and orderly essay.

Now try your hand at the other writing prompts.

Use each of these ideas for writing an essay.

1. We all go through maturing processes. Think of a specific process you have experienced. Then think of something that reflects your process, much like the figs reflect Babette's growth. Write an essay on your own growing up process, relating it to a continuing symbol.

2. Age has an effect on all of us. Write about a specific incident when age affected you or someone you know.

Further Writing

1. Read Kate Chopin's "The Storm" (available in a library), and compare and contrast the images of nature in "The Storm" with those in "Ripe Figs."

2. Read Kate Chopin's "The Kiss" (page 50), and compare Nathalie in "The Kiss" with Calixta in "The Storm."

Answers to 10 Short Questions

6. b. We are clearly told Maman is "patient" and not "impatient."
7. b. We know Babette is the one growing and "maturing."
8. c. Their genteel life, her leisurely breakfast, and the "silver fruit-knife" all imply wealth.
9. b Bayou-Lafourche, in Louisiana, and Maman's reluctance to let Babette go at all both imply that this is, on the one hand, not "near by" and, on the other hand, not "very, very far away." The middle choice is the <u>best</u> choice here.
10. c. Again, we have discussed literary seasons and the middle choice is the <u>best</u> choice here. Spring or summer would refer to youth, and winter would refer to old age. Chrysanthemums bloom in the fall, and fall represents middle age.

Answers to 5 Significant Quotations

2. You should note that this sets up the central tension of Babette having to wait for the figs to ripen so that she can go visiting.
3. You should comment on Babette's "restlessness" and Maman's patience. This is not an easy wait for Babette.
4. You should explain that this is the moment of climax. The figs are ripe. You should explain that the ripe figs represent Babette's maturing and she now is old enough/mature enough/ripe enough to travel to see her cousins.
5. You should note that this is the story's resolution, the dénouement. Babette may now travel.

NOTES

CHAPTER 1

Characters
and Conflicts

Characters are the creatures that create, move, and experience the actions of a story. We normally think of characters as alive, animated beings, such as humans or animals, who can participate in the action. A character may also be called an **actor, player, person, persona**, or **personage**.

Characters fall into two categories: main characters and supporting characters. Generally, a **main character** is central to the action. A **supporting character** may encourage the action and is usually not present as much, or not as central to the action, as the main character. Sometimes, it is difficult to decide if a character is main or supporting. For instance, in a murder mystery the victim may only appear at the beginning of the story or not at all, but the entire story is about solving her or his murder. Is the victim a main character because the entire story is about her or him, or is s/he a supporting character because s/he simply is not present? Both answers may be correct. In literature there are not always so much right or wrong answers as there are explanations, analyses, and debates. The correctness of your answers may depend on how well you explain your choices.

The author speaks to us through her or his characters. When an author writes using "I" or "we," this is called a **first-person narration**. The first-person makes a story very immediate. The character who tells the story is called the **narrator**. If the author addresses the reader directly using "you," this narrative technique is called a **second-person narration**. The second-person is not used often in American literature. Finally, if the author uses "he," "she," "it," or "they" to tell the story, this narrative technique is called a **third-person narration**. This is the most common narrative form, with the author seeming to be more of an observer and less of a participant in the story. In this chapter, "The Kiss" is told in the third person, but "Salvation" and "Eleven" are told in the first person. Notice how

"Salvation" and "Eleven" have such an immediate and different effect on you, the reader.

Characters may also be considered protagonists or antagonists. "Pro" means "for," and the **protagonist** is the hero or heroine, the character we **empathize** with, or share feelings with, the character we root for. "Anti" means "against," and the **antagonist** is the villain, the enemy of the protagonist, the character we do not like, the character we root against. Be aware that authors like to play with these roles. You may be sympathetic to one character and then find that the author turns things upside down and you no longer like the character.

When we talk about protagonists and antagonists, we need to talk about conflicts. **Conflicts** are the disagreements between characters. Conflicts build the tension in a story. Many types of conflicts are possible. The conflict may be **human versus human**, as when a character(s) is pitted against another character(s). Notice the conflict between the narrator and Mrs. Price in "Eleven." The conflict may be **human versus society**, as when a character(s) struggles against a group, community, or social structure. Notice how the narrator struggles with the expectations of his community in "Salvation." The conflict may be **human versus technology**, as when a character(s) struggles with the tools of science or machines of society. The unlit room in "The Kiss" leads to Nathalie's near undoing. The conflict may be **human versus nature**, as when a character(s) battles with the forces of nature. Nathalie's romantic attraction certainly brings her conflict. Finally, the conflict may be **human versus the supernatural**, as when a character(s) vies with God or gods or demons. The narrator certainly has his problems in "Salvation." The conflict may be **human versus herself/himself**, as when a character wrestles with her or his own internal and self-defeating **flaw**. Notice the flaws in Nathalie's assumptions in "The Kiss" and the narrator's internal turmoil in "Eleven." More often than not, a story will contain a combination of these conflicts.

Stories in this chapter focus on characters and are called **character studies**. In a character study, the emphasis is on getting to know each character, and the action of the story is used to help you understand each character better. Langston Hughes takes us through the narrator's dilemma in "Salvation," Sandra Cisneros involves us in the narrator's plight in "Eleven," and Kate Chopin clearly presents Nathalie's conflicts in "The Kiss."

Now it is time to turn to the stories. Enjoy the characters you meet.

Salvation

LANGSTON HUGHES

PRE-READING VOCABULARY
CONTEXT

Use context clues to define these words before reading. Use a dictionary as needed.

1. Stealing, telling lies, harming others, and committing murder are all considered very serious *sins. Sin* means _____.

2. Nick enjoyed the animated *revival meeting* that included lively music and spirited prayer. *Revival meeting* means _____.

3. After becoming a minister, Brian was often the *preacher* in the church on Sunday morning. *Preacher* means _____.

4. When he feels he needs strength, Roger is often found *praying* to St. Anthony to help him. *Praying* means _____.

5. In the Christian religion, *Jesus* is considered the savior of all human-kind. *Jesus* means _____.

6. At the funeral, the children of the person who died were the saddest *mourners. Mourner* means _____.

7. Kind and innocent people are often considered *lambs* because *lambs* are gentle and helpless animals. *Lamb* means _____.

8. Many religions believe that the body of a person dies here on Earth, but the *soul* of that person lives on after death. *Soul* means

_____.

9. Carol worships *God* the almighty Father and Creator every time she goes to church. *God* means _____.

10. When Evelyn walked in the church, she saw the beautiful marble *altar* at the front of the church. *Altar* means _____.

11. Akim went through training and became a *deacon* so that he could help the minister with Sunday services. *Deacon* means

_____.

12. When everyone left and there was no one else in sight, Letisha realized that she was totally *alone*. *Alone* means _____.

13. When everyone arrived at church, the minister then began the ceremony and addressed the whole *congregation*. *Congregation* means

_____.

14. When the airplane was late, Barbara and Sarah ended up *waiting* for another plane to arrive. *Waiting* means _____.

15. After Nala lied to her mother, Nala felt terribly *ashamed* and finally told the truth to get rid of her guilt. *Ashamed* means

_____.

16. Nala realized that telling the truth was much better than *lying*, because *lying* only makes things worse. *Lying* means

_____.

17. Ethan studied long and hard to become a good *minister* so that he could lead his own church. *Minister* means _____.

18. When the queen entered the room, everyone became *hushed* and there was not a sound in the room. *Hushed* means

_____.

19. At the end of the prayer service, the congregation all said "*Amen*," signifying they all agreed. *Amen* means _____.

20. In Christianity, God is the Creator, the Son is the Savior, and the *Holy Ghost* is the Spirit. *Holy Ghost* means _____.

PRE-READING VOCABULARY
STRUCTURAL ATTACK

Define these words by solving the parts. Use the Glossary or a dictionary as needed.

1. hardened
2. sinner
3. rhythmical
4. jet-black
5. work-gnarled
6. proudly
7. rejoicing
8. grinning
9. joyous
10. lied
11. deceived

PRE-READING QUESTIONS

Try answering these questions as you read.

Who is the narrator?

Who is Westley?

Where are they?

What are they supposed to do?

Salvation

Langston Hughes

Langston Hughes was born in Joplin, Missouri, in 1902. After his parents' separation, he spent his early childhood with his grandmother in Lawrence, Kansas. His grandmother gave him a positive outlook on his African American heritage and on life through her stories filled with characters who triumphed over life's problems with zeal and determination. At twelve, he moved back with his mother and lived in Lincoln, Illinois. Later, he served as a crewman on freighters and traveled to Africa, Holland, and Paris. He returned to Washington, D.C., and then moved to New York City. Sharing the same patron with Zora Neale Hurston, he attended Columbia University and eventually became a central figure in the Harlem Renaissance. He died in 1967.

Hughes enjoyed a fruitful writing career. His writings reflect the rhythms of Harlem and the positive attitudes of his grandmother. His poems and short stories are available in many collections.

I was saved from sin when I was going on thirteen. But not really saved. It happened like this. There was a big revival at my Auntie Reed's church. Every night for weeks there had been much preaching, singing, praying, and shouting, some very hardened sinners had been brought to Christ, and the membership of the church had grown by leaps and bounds. Then just before the revival ended, they held a special meeting for children, "to bring the young lambs to the fold." My aunt spoke of it for days ahead. That night I was escorted to the front row and placed on the mourners' bench with all the other young sinners, who had not yet been brought to Jesus.

2   My aunt told me that when you were saved you saw a light, and something happened to you inside! And Jesus came into your life! And God was with you from then on! She said you could see and hear and feel Jesus in your soul. I believed her. I had heard a great many old people say the same thing and it seemed to me they ought to know. So I sat there calmly in the hot, crowded church, waiting for Jesus to come to me.

3   The preacher preached a wonderful rhythmical sermon, all moans and shouts and lonely cries and dire pictures of hell, and then he sang a song about the ninety and nine safe in the fold, but one little lamb was left out in the cold. Then he said: "Won't you come? Won't you come to Jesus? Young lambs, won't you come?" And he held out his arms to all us young sinners there on the mourners' bench. And the little girls cried. And some of them jumped up and went to Jesus right away. But most of us just sat there.

4   A great many old people came and knelt around us and prayed, old women with jet-black faces and braided hair, old men with work-gnarled hands. And the church sang a song about the lower lights are burning, some poor sinners to be saved. And the whole building rocked with prayer and song.

5   Still I kept waiting to *see* Jesus.

6   Finally all the young people had gone to the altar and were saved, but one boy and me. He was a rounder's son named Westley. Westley and I were surrounded by sisters and deacons praying. It was very hot in the church, and getting late now. Finally Westley said to me in a whisper: "God damn! I'm tired o' sitting here. Let's get up and be saved." So he got up and was saved.

7   Then I was left all alone on the mourners' bench. My aunt came and knelt at my knees and cried, while prayers and songs swirled all around me in the little church. The whole congregation prayed for me alone, in a mighty wail of moans and voices. And I kept waiting serenely for Jesus, waiting, waiting—but he didn't come. I wanted to see him, but nothing happened to me. Nothing! I wanted something to happen to me, but nothing happened.

8   I heard the songs and the minister saying: "Why don't you come? My dear child, why don't you come to Jesus? Jesus is waiting for you. He wants you. Why don't you come? Sister Reed, what is this child's name?"

9   "Langston," my aunt sobbed.

10   "Langston, why don't you come? Why don't you come and be saved? Oh, Lamb of God! Why don't you come?"

11   Now it was really getting late. I began to be ashamed of myself, holding everything up so long. I began to wonder what God thought about Westley, who certainly hadn't seen Jesus either, but who was now sitting proudly on the platform, swinging his knickerbockered legs and grinning down at me, surrounded by deacons and old women on their knees praying. God had not struck Westley dead for taking his name in vain or for lying in the temple. So I decided that maybe to save further trouble, I'd better lie, too, and say that Jesus had come, and get up and be saved.

12   So I got up.

13   Suddenly the whole room broke into a sea of shouting, as they saw me rise. Waves of rejoicing swept the place. Women leaped in the air. My aunt threw her arms around me. The minister took me by the hand and led me to the platform.

14   When things quieted down, in a hushed silence, punctuated by a few ecstatic "Amens," all the new young lambs were blessed in the name of God. Then joyous singing filled the room.

15   That night, for the last time in my life but one—for I was a big boy twelve years old—I cried. I cried, in bed alone, and couldn't stop. I buried my head under the quilts, but my aunt heard me. She woke up and told my uncle I was crying because the Holy Ghost had come into my life, and because I had seen Jesus. But I was really crying because I couldn't bear to tell her that I had lied, that I had deceived everybody in the church, that I hadn't seen Jesus, and that now I didn't believe there was a Jesus any more, since he didn't come to help me.

Salvation

JOURNAL

1. **MLA Works Cited**   *Using this model, record this story here.*

   Author's Last Name, First Name. "Title of the Story." *Title of the Book.*

   2nd ed. Ed. First Name Last Name. City: Publisher, year. Page number(s) of

   this story. Print.

2. **Main Character(s)**   *Describe each main character, and explain why you think each is a main character.*

3. **Supporting Characters**   *Describe each supporting character, and explain why you think each is a supporting character.*

4. **Setting and Props**   *Describe the setting(s) and any relevant prop(s).*

5. **Sequence**   *Outline the events of the story in order.*

6. **Plot**   *Tell the story in no more than two sentences.*

7. **Conflicts**   *Identify and explain all the conflicts involved here.*

8. **Significant Quotations**   *Explain the importance of each of these quotations. Record the page number in the parentheses.*

   a. "There was a big revival meeting at my Auntie Reed's church" (   ).

   b. "My aunt told me that when you were saved you saw a light, and something happened to you inside!" (   ).

   c. "Then he said: 'Won't you come? Won't you come to Jesus?'" (   ).

d. "Finally all the young people had gone to the altar and were saved [...]" ( ).

e. "Waves of rejoicing swept the place" ( ).

9. **Literary Elements** *Look at this chapter's title and explain why you think this story is placed in this chapter. Explain in which other chapter(s) you might place this story, as relevant to the literary element(s) of that chapter.*

10. **Foreshadowing, Irony, and/or Symbolism** *Explain examples of foreshadowing, irony, and/or symbolism in this story.*

Follow-up Questions

10 Short Questions

What is the <u>best</u> answer for each?

_____ 1. The narrator and the author are probably
   a. different people.
   b. relatives.
   c. the same person.

_____ 2. This occasion is probably
   a. a religious ceremony.
   b. a school graduation.
   c. a birthday party.

_____ 3. The narrator probably lives with
   a. his parents.
   b. Westley.
   c. his aunt.

_____ 4. In this story, sinners need
   a. to stay the same.
   b. to change.
   c. to sing.

_____ 5. The narrator feels he needs
   a. to hear God.
   b. to see God.
   c. to feel God.

_____ 6. Compared to the girls, the boys
   a. take longer.
   b. take less time.
   c. take the same amount of time.

_____ 7. "Lambs" refers to
   a. the children to be saved.
   b. the older people.
   c. the minister.

_____ 8. The ceremony is generally
   a. very quiet.
   b. very active.
   c. very reserved.

_____ 9. In the end, Westley
   a. does see God.
   b. does feel God.
   c. lies about seeing God.

_____ 10. In the end, the narrator
   a. does see God.
   b. does feel God.
   c. lies about seeing God.

5 Significant Quotations

What is the importance of each of these quotations?

1. "That night I was escorted to the front row and placed on the mourners' bench with all the other young sinners, who had not yet been brought to Jesus."

2. "She said you could see and hear and feel Jesus in your soul. I believed her."

3. "Westley and I were surrounded by sisters and deacons praying."

4. "Suddenly the whole room broke into a sea of shouting, as they saw me rise."

5. "That night, for the last time in my life but one—for I was a big boy twelve years old—I cried."

2 COMPREHENSION ESSAY QUESTIONS

Use specific details and information from the story to answer these questions as completely as possible.

1. How would you describe the narrator's experience? Use specific details and information from the story to support your answer.

2. What significant roles do the setting and the supporting characters play? Use specific details and information from the story to support your answer.

DISCUSSION QUESTIONS

Be prepared to discuss these questions in class.

1. When have you told a lie to get yourself out of a difficult position? How is your experience similar to or different from the narrator's experience?

2. What are the ironies in this story? Use specific details from the story to support your thinking.

WRITING

Use each of these ideas for writing an essay.

1. Discuss a time when you have been expected to do more—or less— than you could do, and discuss the results of that unmet expectation.

2. Discuss a spiritual experience you have had or someone you know has had, and discuss the results of that experience.

Further Writing

1. Research evangelistic religions and the impact of congregations and rituals on their members' conduct and beliefs.

2. Research religious passage rites among either mainstream and/or tribal religions.

Eleven

SANDRA CISNEROS

PRE-READING VOCABULARY
CONTEXT

Use context clues to define these words before reading. Use a dictionary as needed.

1. In order to *understand* why Dan did so many exercises, Flora did just as many exercises and then felt great afterwards. *Understand* means

    _____.

2. Each year, to remember the day Isabel was born her family takes her out for a *birthday* dinner. *Birthday* means _____.

3. Washing the car knowing it is going to rain is a *stupid* idea. *Stupid* means _____.

4. When the little two-year-old hurt himself, he ran to his sitting mother and crawled up to sit in her *lap* to be next to her. *Lap* means

    _____.

5. The penthouse is at the top of the building and every other floor comes before and is *underneath* the penthouse. *Underneath* means

    _____.

6. Jen took out an *onion* to cook for dinner and peeled away all the outer layers until she got to the sweet middle. *Onion* means

    _____.

7. When he scraped his finger, Miguel got out the metal *Band-Aid box* and took out a bandage to cover his scrape. *Band-Aid box* means

    _____.

8. When it turned colder out, Lusumba put on a wool *sweater* over his shirt and buttoned up the buttons to feel warmer. *Sweater* means

    _____.

9. After Delia put stones in a tin can, she shook the can and the stones *rattled* around inside making clinking sounds. *Rattle* means

    _____.

10. For Halloween, the beautiful Dodee put on heavy makeup, a ragged dress, and an old wig to become an *ugly* witch. *Ugly* means

    _____.

11. Two little girls stood away from each other, each holding an end of the rope, and then started swinging the rope around so their friend could hop in and play *jump rope* before the rope hit the ground. *Jump rope* means _____.

12. Rather than taking the main road, Kirk decided to try a shortcut and walked down the narrow *alley* between the buildings. *Alley* means

    _____.

13. In order to avoid her getting splashed when the car drove through the puddle, the man *shoved* the woman to the side to keep her dry. *Shove* means _____.

14. To stay on her diet, Gabriella went to the dairy section in the supermarket and bought the mushy-looking *cottage cheese*. *Cottage cheese* means _____.

15. When Amar hid the new shoes in the back of the closet, the shoes became *invisible* and absolutely impossible to see. *Invisible* means

    _____.

16. After drinking the soda too fast, Elyse got *hiccups* and made strange, hick-hick sounds until the *hiccups* went away. *Hiccups* means

    _____.

17. Sometimes, little Alex likes to *pretend* he is a pirate and runs around with a rubber sword saying, "Ahoy, matey." *Pretend* means

    _____.

18. For her birthday, Heather received many brightly wrapped *presents,* all beautiful gifts tied with colorful ribbons. *Present* means

_____ .

19. When the storm knocked the power out and all the lights went out, we lit a lot of *candles* so we could have some light in the house. *Candle* means _____ .

20. For the party, Laura had all kinds of colorful *balloons* blown up that floated above each table. *Balloon* means _____ .

PRE-READING VOCABULARY STRUCTURAL ATTACK

Define these words by solving the parts. Use the Glossary or a dictionary as needed.

 1. yesterday
 2. wooden
 3. coatroom
 4. somebody
 5. skinny
 6. raggedy
 7. lunchtime
 8. schoolyard
 9. itchy
10. everybody
11. clown-sweater
12. dumber
13. runaway

PRE-READING QUESTIONS

Try answering these questions as you read.

What is special about this day?

How old is the narrator?

What happens to the narrator?

How does the narrator feel about her age?

Eleven

SANDRA CISNEROS

Sandra Cisneros was born in Chicago in 1954 to a father of Mexican heritage and a mother of Mexican American heritage. Cisneros has served as a high school teacher, a college recruiter, an art administrator, and a collegiate visiting writer. She has also received NEA fellowships for both fiction and poetry. Her writing insightfully looks inward and can be found in short story and poetry collections. *The House on Mango Street* is her most noted novel.

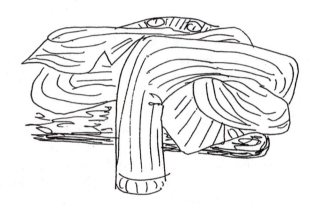

What they don't understand about birthdays and what they never tell you is that when you're eleven, you're also ten, and nine, and eight, and seven, and six, and five, and four, and three, and two, and one. And when you wake up on your eleventh birthday you expect to feel eleven, but you don't. You open your eyes and everything's just like yesterday, only it's today. And you don't feel eleven at all. You feel like you're still ten. And you are—underneath the year that makes you eleven.

2   Like some days you might say something stupid, and that's the part of you that's still ten. Or maybe some days you might need to sit on your mama's lap because you're scared, and that's the part of you that's five. And maybe one day when you're all grown up maybe you will need to cry like if you're three, and that's okay. That's what I tell Mama when she's sad and needs to cry. Maybe she's feeling three.

3   Because the way you grow old is kind of like an onion or like the rings inside a tree trunk or like my little wooden dolls that fit one inside the other, each year inside the next one. That's how being eleven years old is.

4   You don't feel eleven. Not right away. It takes a few days, weeks even, sometimes even months before you say Eleven when they ask you. And you don't feel smart eleven, not until you're almost twelve. That's the way it is.

5   Only today I wish I didn't have only eleven years rattling inside me like pennies in a tin Band-Aid box. Today I wish I was one hundred and two instead of eleven because if I was one hundred and two I'd have known what to say when Mrs. Price put the red sweater on my desk. I would've known how to tell her it wasn't mine instead of just sitting there with that look on my face and nothing coming out of my mouth.

6   "Whose is this?" Mrs. Price says, and she holds the red sweater up in the air for all the class to see. "Whose? It's been sitting in the coat-room for a month."

7   "Not mine," says everybody. "Not me."

8   "It has to belong to somebody," Mrs. Price keeps saying, but nobody can remember. It's an ugly sweater with red plastic buttons and a collar and sleeves all stretched out like you could use it for a jump rope. It's maybe a thousand years old and even if it belonged to me I wouldn't say so.

9   Maybe because I'm skinny, maybe because she doesn't like me, that stupid Sylvia Saldivar says, "I think it belongs to Rachel." An ugly sweater like that, all raggedy and old, but Mrs. Price believes her. Mrs. Price takes the sweater and puts it right on my desk, but when I open my mouth nothing comes out.

10   "That's not, I don't, you're not... Not mine," I finally say in a little voice that was maybe me when I was four.

11   "Of course it's yours," Mrs. Price says. "I remember you wearing it once." Because she's older and the teacher, she's right and I'm not.

12   Not mine, not mine, not mine, but Mrs. Price is already turning to page thirty-two, and math problem number four. I don't know why but all of a sudden I'm feeling sick inside, like the part of me that's three wants to come out of my eyes, only I squeeze them shut tight and bite down on my teeth real hard and try to remember today I am eleven, eleven. Mama is making a cake for me for tonight, and when Papa comes home everybody will sing Happy birthday, happy birthday to you.

13   But when the sick feeling goes away and I open my eyes, the red sweater's still sitting there like a big red mountain. I move the red sweater to the corner of my desk with my ruler. I move my pencil and books and eraser as far from it as possible. I even move my chair a little to the right. Not mine, not mine, not mine.

14   In my head I'm thinking how long till lunchtime, how long till I can take the red sweater and throw it over the schoolyard fence, or

leave it hanging on a parking meter, or bunch it up into a little ball and toss it in the alley. Except when math period ends Mrs. Price says loud and in front of everybody, "Now, Rachel, that's enough," because she sees I've shoved the red sweater to the tippy-tip corner of my desk and it's hanging all over the edge like a waterfall, but I don't care.

15   "Rachel," Mrs. Price says. She says it like she's getting mad. "You put that sweater on right now and no more nonsense."

16   "But it's not—"

17   "Now!" Mrs. Price says.

18   This is when I wish I wasn't eleven, because all the years inside of me—ten, nine, eight, seven, six, five, four, three, two, and one—are pushing at the back of my eyes when I put one arm through one sleeve of the sweater that smells like cottage cheese, and then the other arm through the other and stand there with my arms apart like if the sweater hurts me and it does, all itchy and full of germs that aren't even mine.

19   That's when everything I've been holding in since this morning, since when Mrs. Price put the sweater on my desk, finally lets go, and all of a sudden I'm crying in front of everybody. I wish I was invisible but I'm not. I'm eleven and it's my birthday today and I'm crying like I'm three in front of everybody. I put my head down on the desk and bury my face in my stupid clown-sweater arms. My face all hot and spit coming out of my mouth because I can't stop the little animal noises from coming out of me, until there aren't any more tears left in my eyes, and it's just my body shaking like when you have the hiccups, and my whole head hurts like when you drink milk too fast.

20   But the worst part is right before the bell rings for lunch. That stupid Phyllis Lopez, who is even dumber than Sylvia Saldivar, says she remembers the red sweater is hers! I take it off right away and give it to her, only Mrs. Price pretends like everything's okay.

21   Today I'm eleven. There's a cake Mama's making for tonight, and when Papa comes home from work we'll eat it. There'll be candles and presents and everybody will sing Happy birthday, happy birthday to you, Rachel, only it's too late.

22   I'm eleven today. I'm eleven, ten, nine, eight, seven, six, five, four, three, two, and one, but I wish I was *one hundred* and two. I wish I was anything but eleven, because I want today to be far away already, far away like a runaway balloon, like a tiny *o* in the sky, so tiny-tiny you have to close your eyes to see it.

Eleven

Journal

1. **MLA Works Cited**   *Using this model, record this story here.*

    Author's Last Name, First Name. "Title of the Story" *Title of the Book.*

    2nd ed. Ed. First Name Last Name. City: Publisher, year. Page number(s) of

    this story. Print.

2. **Main Character(s)**   *Describe each main character, and explain why you think each is a main character.*

3. **Supporting Characters**   *Describe each supporting character, and explain why you think each is a supporting character.*

4. **Setting and Props**   *Describe the setting(s) and any relevant prop(s).*

5. **Sequence**   *Outline the events of this story in order.*

6. **Plot**   *Tell the story in no more than two sentences.*

7. **Conflicts**   *Identify and explain all the conflicts involved here.*

8. **Significant Quotations**   *Explain the importance of each of these quotations. Record the page number in the parentheses.*

   a. "You feel like you're still ten" (   ).

   b. "Or maybe some days you might need to sit on your mama's lap because you're scared, and that's the part of you that's five" (   ).

   c. "Maybe because I'm skinny, maybe because she doesn't like me, that stupid Sylvia Saldivar says, 'I think it belongs to Rachel'" (   ).

d. "I'm eleven and it's my birthday today and I'm crying like I'm three in front of everybody" (   ).

e. "That stupid Phyllis Lopez, who is even dumber than Sylvia Saldivar, says she remembers the red sweater is hers" (   ).

9. **Literary Elements**   *Look at this chapter's title and explain why you think this story is placed in this chapter. Explain in which other chapter(s) you might place this story, as relevant to the literary element(s) of that chapter.*

10. **Foreshadowing, Irony, and/or Symbolism**   *Explain examples of foreshadowing, irony, and/or symbolism in this story.*

Follow-up Questions

10 Short Questions

*What is the **best** answer for each?*

_____ 1. The narrator is
  a. male.
  b. female.
  c. old.

_____ 2. The narrator seems to
  a. like being eleven.
  b. not like being eleven.
  c. not care about being eleven.

_____ 3. The narrator feels each birthday
  a. is special.
  b. is important.
  c. is the sum of prior birthdays.

_____ 4. The narrator
  a. recognizes the sweater.
  b. likes the sweater.
  c. does not want the sweater.

_____ 5. The sweater is
  a. unattractive.
  b. attractive.
  c. new.

_____ 6. The sweater has been found by
  a. Mrs. Price.

  b. the narrator.
  c. Sylvia Saldivar.

_____ 7. The person who insists it is the narrator's sweater is
  a. Mrs. Price.
  b. the narrator.
  c. Phyllis Lopez.

_____ 8. For the narrator, the sweater is
  a. unimportant.
  b. greatly upsetting.
  c. a nice surprise.

_____ 9. Ultimately, the sweater belongs to
  a. the narrator.
  b. Sylvia Saldivar.
  c. Phyllis Lopez.

_____ 10. In the end, the narrator seems
  a. to be thrilled to celebrate her birthday.
  b. to like being eleven.
  c. not to like being eleven.

5 Significant Quotations

What is the importance of each of these quotations?

1. "And you are—underneath the year that makes you eleven."

2. "And maybe one day when you're all grown up maybe you will need to cry like if you're three, and that's okay."

3. "'Of course it's yours,' Mrs. Price says. 'I remember you wearing it once.'"

4. "[A]nd all of a sudden I'm crying in front of everybody."

5. "I take it off right away and give it to her [Phyllis Lopez], Only Mrs. Price pretends like everything's okay."

2 COMPREHENSION ESSAY QUESTIONS

Use specific details and information from the story to answer these questions as completely as possible.

1. What is the narrator's attitude toward age? Use specific details from the story to explain your answer.

2. What is ironic in this story? Use specific information from the story to explain your answer.

DISCUSSION QUESTIONS

Be prepared to discuss these questions in class.

1. Why do you think the sweater has such a large effect on the narrator? What is something that has affected you this way?

2. How does the narrator feel about aging? How do her ideas apply to you?

WRITING

Use each of these ideas for writing an essay.

1. Age is of great concern to the narrator. Write about a specific time when your age has influenced the way that people have treated you.

2. The sweater causes the narrator a great deal of anxiety, all of which is unnecessary when the sweater turns out to belong to another student. Write about a time when you were unnecessarily upset, relating both the cause and the effect of your discomfort.

Further Writing

1. Ageism has become a concern in the workplace. Research the effects age may have on a career that interests you.

2. People are living longer and longer. Research longevity rates—and the explanations for these rates—within your community, state, country, and/or around the world.

The Kiss

KATE CHOPIN

PRE-READING VOCABULARY
CONTEXT

Use context clues to define these words before reading. Use a dictionary as needed.

1. Little Allison gave her brother, Jacob, a *kiss* on his cheek to thank him for giving her a new Barbie doll. *Kiss* means

   _____.

2. When the sun went down, Michelle lit many candles that threw dark but interesting *shadows* on the walls. *Shadow* means

   _____.

3. George found it very hard to read his reports in poor lighting, because nothing was clear in the dark *obscurity*. *Obscurity* means

   _____.

4. Robert and Kristyl are *ardent* readers and go to Walden Books, Barnes and Noble, or the library every chance they get. *Ardent* means

   _____.

5. Laura and Dave are constant *companions*, going everywhere and doing everything together. *Companion* means

   _____.

6. José is very open and honest and is quite *guileless*, so he does not understand when people try to plan and scheme. *Guileless* means

   _____.

7. John is *enormously* talented and can draw anything to look life-like, from animals to people to scenery. *Enormous* means

   _____.

8. To entertain guests after his graduation, Teddy planned a beautiful *reception* at a country club overlooking a golf course. *Reception* means _____.

9. Alice and Tom still enjoy *lingering* memories of their trip to Hawaii every time they look back over the trip's pictures. *Lingering* means

_____.

10. Missy had some *confusion* over which room to go to for specific courses, so she got out her course schedule. *Confusion* means

_____.

11. When the professor called on her, Christina was so surprised she stuttered and *stammered* and did not know what to say. *Stammer* means

_____.

12. Renee found the movie very *comical* and still laughs whenever she thinks about it. *Comical* means _____.

13. Losing someone or something you are close to can bring real and sorrowful *misery*. *Misery* means _____.

14. Lisa called Alex back instead of Ali, because the phone message was not clear and she *misinterpreted* the name. *Misinterpret* means

_____.

15. All dressed in turquoise silk with aquamarines for jewels, Margaret looked *radiant* at her daughter's wedding. *Radiant* means

_____.

16. Dodee and Rich felt *triumphant* when they won the bid on the new house they wanted to buy so badly. *Triumphant* means

_____.

17. Ashley and Caitlin *blush* with rosy red cheeks whenever they run around and get warm. *Blush* means _____.

18. Mark was so *insolent* and nasty to his mother that I would have grounded him for a month. *Insolent* means _____.

19. Playing chess, Carrie and Reid are able to plan and control every move and are accomplished *chess players*. *Chess players* means

_____.

20. Bob, Geri, and Anthony always thank people for helping them and are never *ungrateful* to anyone. *Ungrateful* means

_____.

PRE-READING VOCABULARY
STRUCTURAL ATTACK

Define these words by solving the parts. Use the Glossary or a dictionary as needed.

1. uncertain
2. overtaken
3. newcomer
4. angrily
5. self-justification

6. unavoidable
7. uncomfortable
8. misinterpreted
9. unreasonable

PRE-READING QUESTIONS

Try answering these questions as you read.

What does Mr. Harvy do?

What does Miss Nathalie do?

What does Mr. Brantain do?

The Kiss

KATE CHOPIN

Kate O'Flaherty Chopin was born in St. Louis, Missouri, in 1851 to an affluent family. Although her father died when she was young, her widowed mother gave young Kate a taste of female independence. In 1870 Kate married Oscar Chopin and moved to New Orleans and then Natchitoches Parish. Here she met the Creoles, Acadians, and African Americans she would later write about. Oscar died in 1882, and by 1884 she sold the plantation, gathered her five children, and returned home to St. Louis, where she began to write and where her works were published in popular women's magazines. Influenced noticeably by Guy de Maupassant's sense of irony and Henrik Ibsen's social comment, Chopin wrote stories, often touched with rich symbols and images of nature, that question societal assumptions and dictates. *The Awakening* remains her masterwork, although short stories offer Chopin at her most terse. Chopin died in 1904.

It was still quite light out of doors, but inside with the curtains drawn and the smouldering fire sending out a dim, uncertain glow, the room was full of deep shadows.

2   Brantain sat in one of these shadows; it had overtaken him and he did not mind. The obscurity lent him courage to keep his eyes fastened as ardently as he liked upon the girl who sat in the firelight.

3   She was very handsome, with a certain fine, rich coloring that belongs to the healthy brune type. She was quite composed, as she idly stroked the satiny coat of the cat that lay curled in her lap, and she occasionally sent a slow glance into the shadow where her companion sat. They were talking low, of indifferent things which plainly were not the things that occupied their thoughts. She knew that he loved

her—a frank, blustering fellow without guile enough to conceal his feelings, and no desire to do so. For two weeks past he had sought her society eagerly and persistently. She was confidently waiting for him to declare himself and she meant to accept him. The rather insignificant and unattractive Brantain was enormously rich; and she liked and required the entourage which wealth could give her.

4   During one of the pauses between their talk of the last tea and the next reception the door opened and a young man entered whom Brantain knew quite well. The girl turned her face toward him. A stride or two brought him to her side, and bending over her chair—before she could suspect his intention, for she did not realize that he had not seen her visitor—he pressed an ardent, lingering kiss upon her lips.

5   Brantain slowly arose; so did the girl arise, but quickly, and the newcomer stood between them, a little amusement and some defiance struggling with the confusion in his face.

6   "I believe," stammered Brantain, "I see that I have stayed too long. I—I had no idea—that is, I must wish you good-by." He was clutching his hat with both hands, and probably did not perceive that she was extending her hand to him, her presence of mind had not completely deserted her; but she could not have trusted herself to speak.

7   "Hang me if I saw him sitting there, Nattie! I know it's deuced awkward for you. But I hope you'll forgive me this once—this very first break. Why, what's the matter?"

8   "Don't touch me; don't come near me," she returned angrily. "What do you mean by entering the house without ringing?"

9   "I came in with your brother, as I often do," he answered coldly, in self-justification. "We came in the side way. He went upstairs and I came in here hoping to find you. The explanation is simple enough and ought to satisfy you that the misadventure was unavoidable. But do say that you forgive me, Nathalie," he entreated, softening.

10   "Forgive you! You don't know what you are talking about. Let me pass. It depends upon—a good deal whether I forgive you."

11   At that next reception which she and Brantain had been talking about she approached the young man with a delicious frankness of manner when she saw him there.

12   "Will you let me speak to you a moment or two, Mr. Brantain?" she asked with an engaging but perturbed smile. He seemed extremely unhappy; but when she took his arm and walked away with him, seeking a retired corner, a ray of hope mingled with the almost comical misery of his expression. She was apparently very outspoken.

13   "Perhaps I should not have sought this interview, Mr. Brantain; but—but, oh, I have been very uncomfortable, almost miserable since that little encounter the other afternoon. When I thought how you

might have misinterpreted it, and believed things"—hope was plainly gaining the ascendancy over misery in Brantain's round, guileless face—"of course, I know it is nothing to you, but for my own sake I do want you to understand that Mr. Harvy is an intimate friend of long standing. Why, we have always been like cousins—like brother and sister, I may say. He is my brother's most intimate associate and often fancies that he is entitled to the same privileges as the family. Oh, I know it is absurd, uncalled for, to tell you this; undignified even," she was almost weeping, "but it makes so much difference to me what you think of—me." Her voice had grown very low and agitated. The misery had all disappeared from Brantain's face.

14   "Then you do really care what I think, Miss Nathalie? May I call you Miss Nathalie?" They turned into a long, dim corridor that was lined on either side with tall, graceful plants. They walked slowly to the very end of it. When they turned to retrace their steps Brantain's face was radiant and hers was triumphant.

15   Harvy was among the guests at the wedding; and he sought her out in a rare moment when she stood alone.

16   "Your husband," he said, smiling, "has sent me over to kiss you."

17   A quick blush suffused her face and round polished throat. "I suppose it's natural for a man to feel and act generously on an occasion of this kind. He tells me he doesn't want his marriage to interrupt wholly that pleasant intimacy which has existed between you and me. I don't know what you've been telling him," with an insolent smile, "but he has sent me here to kiss you."

18   She felt like a chess player who, by the clever handling of his pieces, sees the game taking the course intended. Her eyes were bright and tender with a smile as they glanced up into his; and her lips looked hungry for the kiss which they invited.

19   "But, you know," he went on quietly, "I didn't tell him so, it would have seemed ungrateful, but I can tell you. I've stopped kissing women; it's dangerous."

20   Well, she had Brantain and his million left. A person can't have everything in this world; and it was a little unreasonable of her to expect it.

The Kiss

JOURNAL

1. **MLA Works Cited**   *Using this model, record this story here.*

    Author's Last Name, First Name. "Title of the Story." *Title of the Book.*

    2nd ed. Ed. First Name Last Name. City: Publisher, year. Page number(s)

    of this story. Print.

2. **Main Character(s)**   *Describe each main character, and explain why you think each is a main character.*

3. **Supporting Characters**   *Describe each supporting character, and explain why you think each is a supporting character.*

4. **Setting and Props**   *Describe the setting(s) and any relevant prop(s).*

5. **Sequence**   *Outline the events of the story in order.*

6. **Plot**   *Tell the story in no more than two sentences.*

7. **Conflicts**   *Identify and explain all the conflicts involved here.*

8. **Significant Quotations**   *Explain the importance of each quotation completely. Record the page number in the parentheses.*

   a. "Brantain sat in one of those shadows; it had overtaken him and he did not mind" (   ).

   b. "A stride or two brought him to her side, and bending over her chair—before she could suspect his intention, for she did not realize that he had not seen her visitor—he pressed an ardent, lingering kiss upon her lips" (   ).

   c. " 'Don't touch me; don't come near me,' she returned angrily" (   ).

   d. " 'Why, we have always been like cousins—like brother and sister' " (   ).

e. "She felt like a chess player who, by the clever handling of his pieces, sees the game taking the course intended" (   ).

9. **Literary Elements**   *Look at this chapter's title and explain why you think this story is placed in this chapter. Explain in which other chapter(s) you might place this story, as relevant to the literary element(s) of the chapter(s).*

10. **Foreshadowing, Irony, and/or Symbolism**   *Explain examples of foreshadowing, irony, and/or symbolism in this story.*

Follow-up Questions

10 SHORT QUESTIONS

What is the __best__ answer for each?

1. Nathalie
   a. knows Brantain is in the shadows.
   b. does not know Brantain is seated in the shadows.
   c. has not yet met Brantain.

2. Nathalie
   a. knows Brantain is rich.
   b. has no idea of Brantain's wealth.
   c. does not care about Brantain's wealth.

3. At that moment, Nathalie
   a. expects Harvy to kiss her.
   b. is happy Harvy kisses her.
   c. is caught off guard by the kiss.

4. Brantain
   a. is upset by the kiss.
   b. does not see the kiss.
   c. does not care about the kiss.

5. Harvy
   a. knows Brantain is there.
   b. does not know Brantain is there.
   c. does not care if Brantain is there.

6. Harvy kissing Nathalie
   a. does not upset Brantain.
   b. probably has never happened before.
   c. probably has happened before.

7. Brantain
   a. stays.
   b. leaves.
   c. is not there.

8. Later, Nathalie
   a. says she loves Harvy.
   b. ignores the kiss.
   c. blames the kiss on Harvy.

9. Ultimately, Brantain
   a. leaves Nathalie.
   b. marries Nathalie.
   c. shoots Harvy.

10. Ultimately, Nathalie seems
    a. to love Brantain deeply.
    b. to want to marry Harvy desperately.
    c. to have wanted both love and money.

5 SIGNIFICANT QUOTATIONS

What is the importance of each quotation?

1. "The obscurity lent him courage to keep his eyes fastened as ardently as he liked upon the girl who sat in the firelight."

2. "A stride or two brought him to her side; and bending over her chair—before she could suspect his intention, for she did not realize that he had not seen her visitor—he pressed an ardent, lingering kiss upon her lips."

3. "'Hang me if I saw him sitting there, Nattie! I know it's deuced awkward for you.'"

4. "'When I thought how you might have misinterpreted it, and believed things—[…].'"

5. "Her eyes were bright and tender with a smile as they glanced up into his; and her lips looked hungry for the kiss which they invited."

2 COMPREHENSION ESSAY QUESTIONS

Use specific details and information from the story to answer these questions as completely as possible.

1. How does the title relate to the story? Use specific details and information from the story to substantiate your answer.

2. What roles do the settings play in this story? Use specific details and information from the story to substantiate your answer.

DISCUSSION QUESTIONS

Be prepared to discuss these questions in class.

1. How do you feel about Nathalie? Brantain? Harvy?

2. Who is the protagonist here? The antagonist?

WRITING

Use each of these ideas for writing an essay.

1. There is certainly a good deal of deception and manipulation going on in this story. Think of a time you or someone you know deceived or manipulated someone else. Describe the deception or manipulation and the consequences of that behavior.

2. There is also a good deal of insincerity in this story. Describe a time you or someone you know was fooled by someone else's insincerity.

Further Writing

1. Read "The Story of an Hour" by Kate Chopin (page 159) and compare Nathalie with Louise Mallard and Brantain with Brently Mallard.

2. Read "An Embarrassing Position" by Kate Chopin (available in a library) and compare Nathalie with Eva Artless and Brantain with Willis Parkham.

NOTES

CHAPTER 2

Setting and Props

Setting is the catch-all term that describes the time, place, and surroundings of a story. The surroundings include the mood and/or tone of the story and even the inanimate objects that support the actions of the story. In a short story, the setting is usually, although not always, limited. The story usually takes place in a shorter amount of time than in a longer work, and fewer places are involved.

The **time** during which a story takes place may be a historical period, such as the ancient, medieval, or modern period, or it may be an era, such as the Roaring Twenties, the Depression, or a world war. The time period may be a season—spring, summer, winter, or fall—or it may be a rainy, sunny, planting, or harvesting period, or part of a day, such as daytime or nighttime. "Strong Temptations—Strategic Movements—The Innocents Beguiled," for instance, will make more sense to you if you know that it takes place on a beautiful day.

Place is the location where a story is set. That "The Hockey Sweater" is set in Canada, where hockey is the national pastime and where there are difficulties between the French- and English-speaking people, that "Trail of the Green Blazer" takes place in a bazaar, and that "Strong Temptations—Strategic Movements—The Innocents Beguiled" takes place in a small town are all important to the events in the story.

Mood or **tone** sets the general feeling of the story. A bright setting that is filled with sunlight and light breezes sets a much different mood or tone than a decaying, haunted house. Think of setting *Phantom of the Opera* on a bright, sun-filled beach; it would not work. Notice in "The Hockey Sweater" that the author sets a humorous tone for his satirical observations. In "Trail of the Green Blazer" and "Strong Temptations—Strategic Movements—The Innocents Beguiled," the authors again use humor and an even lighter tone to underline each message.

Props (short for "properties") are the inanimate objects in a story. Props are important to recognize and sometimes even take on the qualities of characters. In "The Hockey Sweater," the sweater takes on a life of its own as its effects swirl around the narrator. In "Trail of the Green Blazer," the objects are at the root of Ragu's troubles. And in "Strong Temptations—Strategic Movements—The Innocents Beguiled," the fence and whitewash are absolutely essential to the story.

Enjoy the time and places to which these stories take you.

The Hockey Sweater

ROCH CARRIER

PRE-READING VOCABULARY
CONTEXT

Use context clues to define these words before reading. Use a dictionary as needed.

1. *Hockey* is a game played on ice between two teams that each try to hit a small puck into a net. *Hockey* means _____.

2. For some winter fun, the children took their skates and went to the *skating-rink* to slide on the ice. *Skating-rink* means

   _____.

3. After the criminal robbed the bank, the judge told him he would have to go to prison as *punishment*. *Punishment* means

   _____.

4. The team members all agreed to wear the same clothes in their games, so they all ordered white *uniforms*. *Uniform* means

   _____.

5. Pierre rooted for the *Montreal Canadiens* because they play in his city of Montreal and because they have been hockey champions. *Montreal Canadiens* means _____.

6. When Rich became a *referee*, he had to be on the field for every game and he had to call all of the penalties. *Referee* means

   _____.

7. Ellen gave Matty a *whistle* that he could put in his mouth and blow each time there was a penalty. *Whistle* means

   _____.

8. In hockey, the object of the game is to hit the small, hard, black *puck* into the net to score a goal. *Puck* means

_____.

9. Dodee took out the J.C. Penney *catalogue* and looked at all of the pictures to decide what shoes to order. *Catalogue* means

_____.

10. When Lori is in America she shops at Macy's, but when she is in Canada she shops at *Eaton's*. *Eaton's* means

_____.

11. After planting the fields, Scott went to the *general store* to buy milk, seeds, a sweater, and a blanket. *General store* means

_____.

12. Avani cried and felt much *sorrow* when she learned that her pet cat had died. *Sorrow* means _____.

13. The *Toronto Maple Leafs* is the hockey team that wears the maple leaf that symbolizes the non-French part of Canada. *Toronto Maple Leafs* means _____.

14. Andy's team *trounced* the other team by winning with a score of 65 to 1. *Trounce* means _____.

15. Blowing one's nose in a napkin and burping and belching after dinner is *abominable* behavior. *Abominable* means

_____.

16. In Canada, some people speak English and some speak French; French speakers refer to English speakers as *Anglais*. *Anglais* means

_____.

17. Cheryl, who is a hard worker, felt deeply *insulted* when the consultant told her that she is lazy. *Insulted* means

_____.

18. Early Christians suffered great *persecution* under the Romans and were often tortured or killed. *Persecution* means

_____.

19. Our *vicar*, or pastor, offers religious services at our church every Sunday morning. *Vicar* means

_____.

20. The white *moth*, a relative of the butterfly, flew around the light and looked for a wool blanket to lay its eggs in. *Moth* means

_____.

PRE-READING VOCABULARY STRUCTURAL ATTACK

Define these words by solving the parts. Use the Glossary or a dictionary as needed.

1. daydream
2. schoolteacher
3. disappointment
4. triumphant

PRE-READING QUESTIONS

Try answering these questions as you read.

What does the narrator love to do?

What happens to his old sweater?

What happens because of his new sweater?

The Hockey Sweater

ROCH CARRIER

Roch Carrier was born in 1937. Carrier uses his humor to portray societal tensions in Quebec, Canada. The people of Quebec Province are largely French-speaking, while much of the remaining population of Canada is largely English-speaking. Over the years, the differences in language and cultural heritage have led to various societal tensions and conflicts. In this story, Carrier uses an innocuous piece of clothing to contrast the child's needs with the misunderstandings of the institutions around him. Carrier's masterwork is *La Guerre, Yes Sir!*

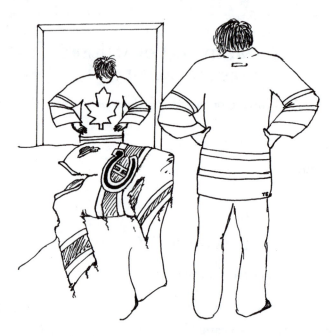

The winters of my childhood were long, long seasons. We lived in three places—the school, the church and the skating-rink—but our real life was on the skating-rink. Real battles were won on the skating-rink. Real strength appeared on the skating-rink. The real leaders showed themselves on the skating-rink. School was a sort of punishment. Parents always want to punish children and school is their most natural way of punishing us. However, school was also a quiet place where we could prepare for the next hockey game, lay out our next strategies. As for church, we found there the tranquility of God: there we forgot school and dreamed about the next hockey game. Through our daydreams it might happen that we would recite a prayer: we would ask God to help us play as well as Maurice Richard.

2   We all wore the same uniform as he, the red, white and blue uniform of the Montreal Canadiens, the best hockey team in the world; we all combed our hair in the same style as Maurice Richard, and to keep it in place we used a sort of glue—a great deal of glue. We laced our skates like Maurice Richard, we taped our sticks like Maurice Richard. We cut all his pictures out of the papers. Truly, we knew everything about him.

3   On the ice, when the referee blew his whistle the two teams would rush at the puck; we were five Maurice Richards taking it away from five other Maurice Richards; we were ten players, all of us wearing with the same blazing enthusiasm the uniform of the Montreal Canadiens. On our backs, we all wore the famous number 9.

4   One day, my Montreal Canadiens sweater had become too small; then it got torn and had holes in it. My mother said: "If you wear that old sweater people are going to think we're poor!" Then she did what she did whenever we needed new clothes. She started to leaf through the catalogue the Eaton company sent us in the mail every year. My mother was proud. She didn't want to buy our clothes at the general store; the only things that were good enough for us were the latest styles from Eaton's catalogue. My mother didn't like the order forms included with the catalogue; they were written in English and she didn't understand a word of it. To order my hockey sweater, she did as she usually did; she took out her writing paper and wrote in her gentle schoolteacher's hand: "Cher Monsieur Eaton, Would you be kind enough to send me a Canadiens' sweater for my son who is ten years old and a little too tall for his age and Docteur Robitaille thinks he's a little too thin? I'm sending you three dollars and please send me what's left if there's anything left. I hope your wrapping will be better than last time."

5   Monsieur Eaton was quick to answer my mother's letter. Two weeks later we received the sweater. That day I had one of the greatest disappointments of my life! I would even say that on that day I experienced a very great sorrow. Instead of the red, white and blue Montreal Canadiens sweater, Monsieur Eaton had sent us a blue and white sweater with a maple leaf on the front—the sweater of the Toronto Maple Leafs. I'd always worn the red, white and blue Montreal Canadiens sweater; all my friends wore the red, white and blue sweater; never had anyone in my village ever worn the Toronto sweater, never had we even seen a Toronto Maple Leafs sweater. Besides, the Toronto team was regularly trounced by the triumphant Canadiens. With tears in my eyes, I found the strength to say:

6   "I'll never wear that uniform."

7   "My boy, first you're going to try it on! If you make up your mind about things before you try, my boy, you won't go very far in this life."

8   My mother had pulled the blue and white Toronto Maple Leafs sweater over my shoulders and already my arms were inside the sleeves. She pulled the sweater down and carefully smoothed all the creases in the abominable maple leaf on which, right in the middle of my chest, were written the words "Toronto Maple Leafs." I wept.

9   "I'll never wear it."

10   "Why not? This sweater fits you ... like a glove."

11   "Maurice Richard would never put it on his back."

12   "You aren't Maurice Richard. Anyway, it isn't what's on your back that counts, it's what you've got inside your head."

13   "You'll never put it in my head to wear a Toronto Maple Leafs sweater."

14   My mother sighed in despair and explained to me:

15   "If you don't keep this sweater which fits you perfectly I'll have to write to Monsieur Eaton and explain that you don't want to wear the Toronto sweater. Monsieur Eaton's an *Anglais.* He'll be insulted because he likes the Maple Leafs. And if he's insulted do you think he'll be in a hurry to answer us? Spring will be here and you won't have played a single game, just because you didn't want to wear that perfectly nice blue sweater."

16   So I was obliged to wear the Maple Leafs sweater. When I arrived on the rink, all the Maurice Richards in red, white and blue came up, one by one, to take a look. When the referee blew his whistle I went to take my usual position. The captain came and warned me I'd be better to stay on the forward line. A few minutes later the second line was called; I jumped onto the ice. The Maple Leafs sweater weighed on my shoulders like a mountain. The captain came and told me to wait; he'd need me later, on defense. By the third period I still hadn't played; one of the defensemen was hit in the nose with a stick and it was bleeding. I jumped on the ice: my moment had come! The referee blew his whistle; he gave me a penalty. He claimed I'd jumped on the ice when there were already five players. That was too much! It was unfair! It was persecution! It was because of my blue sweater! I struck my stick against the ice so hard it broke. Relieved, I bent down to pick up the debris. As I straightened up I saw the young vicar, on skates, before me.

17   "My child," he said, "just because you're wearing a new Toronto Maple Leafs sweater unlike the others, it doesn't mean you're going to make the laws around here. A proper young man doesn't lose his temper. Now take off your skates and go to the church and ask God to forgive you."

18   Wearing my Maple Leafs sweater I went to the church, where I prayed to God; I asked Him to send, as quickly as possible, moths that would eat up my Toronto Maple Leafs sweater.

The Hockey Sweater

JOURNAL

1. **MLA Works Cited**   *Using this model, record this story here.*

   Author's Last Name, First Name. "Title of the Story." *Title of the Book.* 2nd

   ed. Ed. First Name Last Name. City: Publisher, year. Page number(s) of this

   story. Print.

2. **Main Character(s)**   *Describe each main character, and explain why you think each is a main character.*

3. **Supporting Characters**   *Describe each supporting character, and explain why you think each is a supporting character.*

4. **Setting and Props**   *Describe the setting(s) and all relevant prop(s).*

5. **Sequence**   *Outline the events of the story in order.*

6. **Plot**   *Tell the story in no more than two sentences.*

7. **Conflicts**   *Identify and explain all the conflicts involved here.*

8. **Significant Quotations**   *Explain the importance of each quotation completely. Record the page number in the parentheses.*

   a. "Real battles were won on the skating-rink" (   ).

   b. "On the ice, when the referee blew his whistle the two teams would rush at the puck; [...] we were ten players, all of us wearing with the same blazing enthusiasm the uniform of the Montreal Canadiens" (   ).

c. "One day, my Montreal Canadiens sweater had become too small; then it got torn and had holes in it" (   ).

d. "That day I had one of the greatest disappointments of my life!" (   ).

e. "The captain came and told me to wait; he'd need me later, on defense" (   ).

9. **Literary Elements** *Look at this chapter's title and explain why you think this story is placed in this chapter. Explain in which other chapter(s) you might place this story, as relevant to the literary element(s) of the chapter(s).*

10. **Foreshadowing, Irony, and/or Symbols** *Explain examples of foreshadowing, irony, and/or symbols in this story.*

Follow-up Questions

10 SHORT QUESTIONS

What is the best answer for each?

____ 1. The most important place in the narrator's world is
a. school.
b. church.
c. the skating-rink.

____ 2. Church is a place where
a. the narrator prays for peace.
b. the narrator prays for wisdom.
c. the narrator prays for hockey victories.

____ 3. The narrator
a. gets sick of his old sweater.
b. wears out his old sweater.
c. loses his old sweater.

____ 4. The maple leaf symbolizes
a. Toronto.
b. Montreal.
c. Quebec.

____ 5. The narrator roots for
a. the Montreal Canadiens.
b. the Toronto Maple Leafs.
c. the Montreal Maple Leafs.

____ 6. To get the new sweater
a. the narrator's mother goes to Eaton's.
b. the narrator's mother writes Eaton's.
c. the narrator goes to Eaton's.

____ 7. When the new sweater arrives, the narrator is
a. delighted.
b. distressed.
c. unconcerned.

____ 8. The narrator is upset because
a. it is the wrong team's sweater.
b. it is too new.
c. it is too big.

____ 9. Mom feels the new sweater
a. is too big.
b. is just right.
c. is the wrong team's sweater.

____ 10. As a result of the new sweater, the narrator
a. has problems.
b. is respected by his friends.
c. wins the game.

5 SIGNIFICANT QUOTATIONS

What is the importance of each of these quotations?

1. "We lived in three places—the school, the church and the skating-rink—[...]."

2. "We all wore the same uniform as he, the red, white and blue uniform of the Montreal Canadiens [...]."

3. "She started to leaf through the catalogue the Eaton company sent us in the mail every year."

4. "Monsieur Eaton was quick to answer my mother's letter. Two weeks later we received the sweater."

5. "The referee blew his whistle; he gave me a penalty."

2 COMPREHENSION ESSAY QUESTIONS

Use specific details and information from the story to answer these as completely as possible.

1. How is the sweater central to the story? Use specific details and information from the story to support your answer.

2. What are three specific statements or events that are funny in this story? Use specific details and information from the story to support your answer.

DISCUSSION QUESTIONS

Be prepared to discuss these questions in class.

1. What is your favorite team? How would you feel about wearing a rival team's uniform?

2. What are specific statements or events in this story that are funny?

WRITING

Use each of these ideas for writing an essay.

1. Tell about a time you or someone you know has worn the wrong thing, done the wrong thing, or said the wrong thing. Demonstrate the humor and/or discomfort and the consequences of this wrong act.

2. Discuss a team you root for and your feelings for your team. Compare, or contrast, your feelings with those of the narrator.

Further Writing

1. French-speaking Quebec and the remainder of English-speaking Canada have not always agreed. Research recent developments in Canada.

2. Team loyalty can become a problem when fans get carried away. Research recent violence at games, notably European and/or Latin American soccer matches.

Trail of the Green Blazer

R. K. NARAYAN

PRE-READING VOCABULARY
CONTEXT

Use context clues to define these words before reading. Use a dictionary as needed.

1. Anthony decided to buy a navy *blazer* with gold buttons in place of a sport coat. *Blazer* means _____.

2. Raja wore a beautiful silk *sari* that was trimmed in delicate flowers and that flowed in the breeze. *Sari* means _____.

3. In order to sell his baseball cards, Matt rented a *stall* at the flea market and hung a big banner out in front. *Stall* means

   _____.

4. Rudy thought the vase was too expensive, so he *haggled* with the salesperson to lower the price. *Haggle* means _____.

5. The open drawer with all the money in it was an open *invitation* to the thief to steal the money. *Invitation* means

   _____.

6. After tilling the soil and planting the seeds, the poor *peasant* waited for food to grow so he could eat. *Peasant* means

   _____.

7. The boy was a true *idler* and chose to do nothing all day rather than get a job. *Idler* means _____.

8. Americans use dollars and cents to pay for things while some Asians use *annas* and *rupees*. *Anna* and *rupee* mean _____.

9. Thomas was able to connect tiny wires back and forth between his fingers and everyone was amazed at his *deftness*. *Deftness* means

_____.

10. Everyone thought the thief was *reformed* and on his way to becoming an honest man when he stopped stealing. *Reformed* means

_____.

11. When Theo sold shoes, he was paid an extra *commission* on each pair he sold. *Commission* means _____.

12. Even though she knew her brother's toothache hurt him, Christina had to *suppress* a laugh because he looked so funny. *Suppress* means

_____.

13. The little boy cried when he lost the string and his big, round, red *balloon* sailed off into the sky. *Balloon* means _____.

14. When Patrick wants to get away from it all, he tries to find a quiet and *secluded* place where no one can find him. *Secluded* means

_____.

15. Eliot dug a small *well* to find water and put a wooden fence around the hole so no one would fall in. *Well* means _____.

16. Artie was greatly *disappointed* when the wonderful surprise he ordered for Carol arrived late and damaged. *Disappointed* means

_____.

17. Ethan felt such *pity* for the little puppy stuck at the dog pound that he decided to adopt the puppy and take it home. *Pity* means

_____.

18. The snake moved slowly and no one saw it *sidle* up next to the house to wait for darkness and silence. *Sidle* means _____.

19. The dog dropped his head and *cowered* in the corner when he was yelled at for doing something wrong. *Cower* means _____.

20. After years of law school and a successful career, Shirley was appointed the head *magistrate* for legal affairs. *Magistrate* means

_____.

Use context clues from the text to solve this word.

"It had to be finely balanced and calculated—the same sort of calculations as carry a *shikari* through his tracking of game and see him safely home again" (page 76).

Shikari means _____.

PRE-READING VOCABULARY
STRUCTURAL ATTACK

Define these words by solving the parts. Use the Glossary or a dictionary as needed.

1. villagers
2. twosome
3. marketplace
4. loincloth
5. overshadowed
6. involuntarily
7. fondness
8. shopman
9. motherless
10. carelessness
11. unworthy
12. semicircle

PRE-READING QUESTIONS

Try answering these questions as you read.

Who is the Green Blazer?

Who is Raju?

What is Raju doing?

What does Raju then decide to do?

Trail of the Green Blazer

R. K. Narayan

Rasipuram Krishnaswamy (R. K.) Narayan was born in the Indian city of Madras in 1906. Perhaps because his father was an English teacher, Narayan has chosen to write in non-native English. He has become a prolific writer, often focusing on the combination of, and even open confrontation between, people from different walks of life. He is generally sympathetic to the lower classes and social commentary often emerges through his characters and their plights. His writings can be found in numerous novels and short story collections.

The Green Blazer stood out prominently under the bright sun and blue sky. In all that jostling crowd one could not help noticing it. Villagers in shirts and turbans, townsmen in coats and caps, beggars bare-bodied and women in multicolored saris were thronging the narrow passage between the stalls and moving in great confused masses, but still the Green Blazer could not be missed. The jabber and babble of the marketplace was there, as people harangued, disputed prices, haggled or greeted each other; over it all boomed the voice of a Bible-preacher, and when he paused for breath, from another corner the loudspeaker of a health van amplified on malaria and tuberculosis. Over and above it all the Green Blazer seemed to cry out an invitation. Raju could not ignore it. It was not in his nature to ignore such a persistent invitation. He kept himself half-aloof from the crowd; he could not afford to remain completely aloof or keep himself in it too conspicuously. Wherever he might be, he was harrowed by the fear of being spotted by a policeman; today he wore a loincloth and was bare-bodied, and had wound an enormous turban over his head, which overshadowed his face completely, and he hoped that he would be taken for a peasant from a village.

2   He sat on a stack of cast-off banana stalks beside a shop awning and watched the crowd. When he watched a crowd he did it with concentration. It was his professional occupation. Constitutionally he was an idler and had just the amount of energy to watch in a crowd and put his hand into another person's pocket. It was a gamble, of course. Sometimes he got nothing out of a venture, counting himself lucky if he came out with his fingers intact. Sometimes he picked up a fountain pen, and the "receiver" behind the Municipal Office would not offer even four annas for it, and there was always the danger of being traced through it. Raju promised himself that someday he would leave fountain pens alone; he wouldn't touch one even if it were presented to him on a plate; they were too much bother—inky, leaky and next to worthless if one could believe what the receiver said about them. Watches were in the same category, too.

3   What Raju loved most was a nice, bulging purse. If he saw one he picked it up with the greatest deftness. He took the cash in it, flung it far away and went home with the satisfaction that he had done his day's job well. He splashed a little water over his face and hair and tidied himself up before walking down the street again as a normal citizen. He bought sweets, books and slates for his children, and occasionally a jacket-piece for his wife, too. He was not always easy in mind about his wife. When he went home with too much cash, he had always to take care to hide it in an envelope and shove it under a roof tile. Otherwise she asked too many questions and made herself miserable. She liked to believe that he was reformed and earned the cash he showed her as commission; she never bothered to ask what the commissions were for; a commission seemed to her something absolute.

4   Raju jumped down from the banana stack and followed the Green Blazer, always keeping himself three steps behind. It was a nicely calculated distance, acquired by intuition and practise. The distance must not be so much as to obscure the movement of the other's hand to and from his purse, nor so close as to become a nuisance and create suspicion. It had to be finely balanced and calculated—the same sort of calculations as carry a *shikari* through his tracking of game and see him safely home again. Only this hunter's task was more complicated. The hunter in the forest could count his day a success if he laid his quarry flat; but here one had to extract the heart out of the quarry without injuring it.

5   Raju waited patiently, pretending to be examining some rolls of rush mat, while the Green Blazer spent a considerable length of time drinking a coconut at a nearby booth. It looked as though he would not move again at all. After sucking all the milk in the coconut, he seemed to wait interminably for the nut to be split and the soft white kernel scooped out with

a knife. The sight of the white kernel scooped and disappearing into the other's mouth made Raju, too, crave for it. But he suppressed the thought; it would be inept to be spending one's time drinking and eating while one was professionally occupied; the other might slip away and be lost forever.... Raju saw the other take out his black purse and start a debate with the coconut-seller over the price of coconuts. He had a thick, sawing voice which disconcerted Raju. It sounded like the growl of a tiger, but what jungle-hardened hunter ever took a step back because a tiger's growl sent his heart racing involuntarily! The way the other haggled didn't appeal to Raju either; it showed a mean and petty temperament...too much fondness for money. Those were the narrow-minded troublemakers who made endless fuss when a purse was lost....The Green Blazer moved after all. He stopped before a stall flying colored balloons. He bought a balloon after an endless argument with the shopman—a further demonstration of his meanness. He said, "This is for a motherless boy. I have promised it to him. If it bursts or gets lost before I go home, he will cry all night, and I wouldn't like it at all."

6   Raju got his chance when the other passed through a narrow stile, where people were passing four-thick in order to see a wax model of Mahatma Gandhi reading a newspaper.

7   Fifteen minutes later Raju was examining the contents of the purse. He went away to a secluded spot, behind a disused well. Its crumbling parapet seemed to offer an ideal screen for his activities. The purse contained ten rupees in coins and twenty in currency notes and a few annas in nickel. Raju tucked the annas at his waist in his loincloth. "Must give them to some beggars," he reflected generously. There was a blind fellow yelling his life out at the entrance to the fair and nobody seemed to care. People seemed to have lost all sense of sympathy these days. The thirty rupees he bundled into a knot at the end of his turban and wrapped this again round his head. It would see him through the rest of the month. He could lead a clean life for at least a fortnight and take his wife and children to a picture.

8   Now the purse lay limp within the hollow of his hand. It was only left for him to fling it into the well and dust off his hand and then he might walk among princes with equal pride at heart. He peeped into the well. It had a little shallow water at the bottom. The purse might float, and a floating purse could cause the worst troubles on earth. He opened the flap of the purse in order to fill it up with pebbles before drowning it. Now, through the slit at its side, he saw a balloon folded and tucked away. "Oh, this he bought...." He remembered the other's talk about the motherless child. "What a fool to keep this in the purse," Raju reflected. "It is the carelessness of parents that makes young ones suffer," he ruminated angrily. For a moment he paused over a picture

of the growling father returning home and the motherless one waiting at the door for the promised balloon, and this growling man feeling for his purse...and, oh! it was too painful!

9   Raju almost sobbed at the thought of the disappointed child—the motherless boy. There was no one to comfort him. Perhaps this ruffian would beat him if he cried too long. The Green Blazer did not look like one who knew the language of children. Raju was filled with pity at the thought of the young child—perhaps of the same age as his second son. Suppose his wife were dead...(personally it might make things easier for him, he need not conceal his cash under the roof); he overcame this thought as an unworthy side issue. If his wife should die it would make him very sad indeed and tax all his ingenuity to keep his young ones quiet....That motherless boy must have his balloon at any cost, Raju decided. But how? He peeped over the parapet across the intervening space at the far-off crowd. The balloon could not be handed back. The thing to do would be to put it back into the empty purse and slip it into the other's pocket.

10   The Green Blazer was watching the heckling that was going on as the Bible-preacher warmed up to his subject. A semicircle was asking, "Where is your God?" There was a hubbub. Raju sidled up to the Green Blazer. The purse with the balloon (only) tucked into it was in his palm. He'd slip it back into the other's pocket.

11   Raju realized his mistake in a moment. The Green Blazer caught hold of his arm and cried, "Pickpocket!" The hecklers lost interest in the Bible and turned their attention to Raju, who tried to look appropriately outraged. He cried, "Let me go." The other, without giving a clue to what he proposed, shot out his arm and hit him on the cheek. It almost blinded him. For a fraction of a second Raju lost his awareness of where and even who he was. When the dark mist lifted and he was able to regain his vision, the first figure he noticed in the foreground was the Green Blazer, looming, as it seemed, over the whole landscape. His arms were raised ready to strike again. Raju cowered at the sight. He said, "I...I was trying to put back your purse." The other gritted his teeth in fiendish merriment and crushed the bones of his arm. The crowd roared with laughter and badgered him. Somebody hit him again on the head.

12   Even before the Magistrate Raju kept saying, "I was only trying to put back the purse." And everyone laughed. It became a stock joke in the police world. Raju's wife came to see him in jail and said, "You have brought shame on us," and wept.

13   Raju replied indignantly, "Why? I was only trying to put it back."

14   He served his term of eighteen months and came back into the world— not quite decided what he should do with himself. He told himself, "If ever I pick up something again, I shall make sure I don't have to put it back." For now he believed God had gifted the likes of him with only one-way deftness. Those fingers were not meant to put anything back.

Trail of the Green Blazer
Journal

1. **MLA Works Cited**   *Using this model, record this story here.*

   Author's Last Name, First Name. "Title of the Story." *Title of the Book*. 2nd

   ed. Ed. First Name Last Name. City: Publisher, year. Page number(s) of

   this story. Print.

2. **Main Character(s)**   *Describe each main character, and explain why you think each is a main character.*

3. **Supporting Characters**   *Describe each supporting character, and explain why you think each is a supporting character.*

4. **Setting and Props**   *Describe the setting(s) and all relevant prop(s).*

5. **Sequence**   *Outline the events of the story in order.*

6. **Plot**   *Tell the story in no more than two sentences.*

7. **Conflicts**   *Identify and explain all the conflicts involved here.*

8. **Significant Quotations**   *Explain the importance of each quotation completely. Record the page number in the parentheses.*

   a. "The Green Blazer stood out prominently under the bright sun and blue sky" ( ).

   b. "When he went home with too much cash, he had always to take care to hide it in an envelope and shove it under a roof tile" ( ).

c. "He said, 'This is for a motherless boy' " (   ).

d. "Now, through the slit at its side, he saw a balloon folded and tucked away" (   ).

e. "Those fingers were not meant to put anything back" (   ).

9. **Literary Elements**   *Look at this chapter's title and explain why you think this story is placed in this chapter. Explain in which other chapter(s) you might place this story, as relevant to the literary element(s) of the chapter(s).*

10. **Foreshadowing, Irony, and/or Symbols**   *Explain examples of foreshadowing, irony, and/or symbols in this story.*

Follow-up Questions
10 Short Questions

What is the <u>best</u> answer for each?

_____ 1. Raju is
- a. a pickpocket.
- b. an honest family man.
- c. an honest citizen.

_____ 2. The Green Blazer is probably
- a. a native to the bazaar.
- b. a visitor to the bazaar.
- c. a worker's jacket.

_____ 3. The green blazer implies
- a. the person wearing it has money.
- b. the person wearing it is different from the others.
- c. both a. and b.

_____ 4. Raju prefers to find
- a. fountain pens.
- b. watches.
- c. money.

_____ 5. Raju has
- a. just learned how to pick pockets.
- b. picked pockets before.
- c. never picked pockets before.

_____ 6. Raju's wife thinks
- a. Raju has an honest job.
- b. Raju is not reformed.
- c. Raju is still a thief.

_____ 7. At first, the money makes Raju feel
- a. satisfied.
- b. disappointed.
- c. guilty.

_____ 8. Then, the balloon makes Raju feel
- a. satisfied.
- b. disappointed.
- c. guilty.

_____ 9. Raju decides to
- a. throw the purse away.
- b. return the purse and the balloon.
- c. keep the purse and the balloon.

_____ 10. Raju gets in trouble because
- a. he keeps the purse and the balloon.
- b. he throws away the purse and the balloon.
- c. he tries to return the purse and the balloon.

5 Significant Quotations

What is the importance of each of these quotations?

1. "Over and above it all the Green Blazer seemed to cry out an invitation."

2. "She liked to believe that he was reformed and earned the cash he showed her as commission [...]."

3. "Fifteen minutes later Raju was examining the contents of the purse."

4. "Raju almost sobbed at the thought of the disappointed child—the motherless boy."

5. "Raju realized his mistake in a moment."

2 Comprehension Essay Questions

Use specific details and information from the story to answer these questions as completely as possible.

1. How is the title relevant to the story? Use specific details and information from the story to support your answer.

2. What is the role of the balloon in this story? Use specific details and information from the story to support your answer.

Discussion Questions

Be prepared to discuss these questions in class.

1. What is Raju's profession and do you think he is good at it?

2. What is the irony in this story?

Writing

Use each of these ideas for writing an essay.

1. At one time or another, we have all done something wrong and gotten caught. Write about a time that you or someone you know has gotten caught and what the consequences have been.

2. We all have things that we need to change or reform. Tell about one specific thing that you or someone you know has changed, and contrast the old behavior with the new.

Further Writing

1. Compare and contrast Raju with the two desperados in O. Henry's "The Ransom of Red Chief" (available in a library).

2. In some cultures, thieves are very nearly considered an actual social class. Research social class structures in Middle Eastern and/or Asian cultures.

Strong Temptations— Strategic Movements— The Innocents Beguiled

Mark Twain

Pre-reading Vocabulary
Context

Use context clues to define these words before reading. Use a dictionary as needed.

1. The children poured the water in a *bucket* in order to carry the water to the pool. *Bucket* means _____.

2. Ken painted the house using a solution of line and water called *whitewash*. *Whitewash* means _____.

3. The *continents* of Asia, North America, and South America are all enormous land masses. *Continent* means _____.

4. Little Missy and Carrie had a wonderful time playing on the beach and just generally *skylarking* together. *Skylarking* means

   _____.

5. Emanuel was not sure which suit to buy and *wavered* when he was at the counter, still unsure about which to purchase. *Waver* means

   _____.

6. The sad woman looked so *melancholy* after she lost her dog. *Melancholy* means _____.

7. Robert went to *fetch* his mother at the train station. *Fetch* means

   _____.

8. During the cruise, Jane got off the ship to take many exciting *expeditions* ashore. *Expedition* means _____.

9. In an even trade, the boys *exchanged* one baseball glove for another. *Exchange* means _____.

10. Chester improved his *straightened means* when he took a job and finally had money to spend. *Straightened means* means

_____.

11. The idea of painting the lawn's yellow spots green came as a great *inspiration* to Joe. *Inspiration* means _____.

12. During a lazy afternoon of floating around the pool, RoseAnn ran her fingers *tranquilly* and slowly through the water. *Tranquilly* means _____.

13. Helena is a good friend and never *ridicules* or makes fun of any of her friends. *Ridicule* means _____.

14. Pilar was so interested in the book that she became completely *absorbed* and did not notice anything around her. *Absorbed* means _____.

15. You could see the lazy boy's *reluctance* to help with all the work. *Reluctance* means _____.

16. Ali responded with *alacrity* to the wonderful invitation to see Springsteen for free. *Alacrity* means _____.

17. Little children, who are true *innocents*, are so pure and trusting that they believe everyone. *Innocent* means _____.

18. Don has always been able to earn a lot of money; he has never been *poverty-stricken*. *Poverty-stricken* means _____.

19. When Harold won all the money at the poker game, he *bankrupted* the other players. *Bankrupt* means _____.

20. After he took the job, Amar was *obliged* to show up on time. *Obliged* means _____.

PRE-READING VOCABULARY
STRUCTURAL ATTACK

Define these words by solving the parts. Use the Glossary or a dictionary as needed.

1. long-handled
2. topmost
3. steamboat
4. engine-bells

5. hurricane-deck
6. carelessly
7. poverty-stricken
8. passenger-coach

PRE-READING QUESTIONS

Try answering these questions as you read.

What are the "temptations"?

What are the "strategic movements"?

Who are "the innocents"?

What does Tom do?

What does Tom get everyone else to do?

Strong Temptations—
Strategic Movements—
The Innocents Beguiled

MARK TWAIN

Mark Twain was born Samuel Langhorne Clemens in 1835. Growing up in Hannibal, Missouri, he enjoyed a childhood filled with the glamor of riverboats and the mysteries of the Mississippi. His father died when he was twelve, and Clemens became a printer's apprentice. For ten years he set type for newspapers from Iowa to New York. In 1857 he returned to the Mississippi and became a riverboat pilot. With the coming of the Civil War and decreased river traffic, he headed west and became a journalist. While working for a Nevada newspaper, he adopted the name "Mark Twain," a term riverboat crews used in measuring water depth. In 1869 he journeyed to Europe. In 1890 he married Olivia Langdon and they moved to her hometown of Elmira, New York, where they built a sizable estate that, arguably, contributed to his later financial problems. During the 1890s he suffered the loss of his wife and a daughter as well as financial problems. He died in 1910.

Twain developed a uniquely American style, unstifled by European dictates and reflecting the frontier he explored. His happiest works are set in his fictional St. Petersburg, Missouri, and include *Tom Sawyer* and *The Adventures of Huckleberry Finn*. The death of his wife and daughter led to what is generally agreed as darker and more obscure writing, but this story from *Tom Sawyer* is a classic tale recognized as part of American lore, a story of inspired American ingenuity.

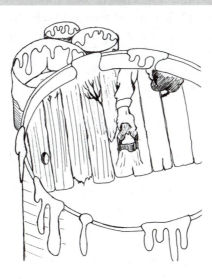

Saturday morning was come, and all the summer world was bright and fresh, and brimming with life. There was a song in every heart; and if the heart was young the music issued at the lips. There was cheer in every face and a spring in every step. The locust trees were in bloom and the fragrance of the blossoms filled the air. Cardiff Hill, beyond the village and above it, was green with vegetation, and it lay just far enough away to seem a Delectable Land, dreamy, reposeful, and inviting.

2   Tom appeared on the sidewalk with a bucket of whitewash and a long-handled brush. He surveyed the fence, and all gladness left him and a deep melancholy settled down upon his spirit. Thirty yards of board fence nine feet high. Life to him seemed hollow, and existence but a burden. Sighing he dipped his brush and passed it along the topmost plank; repeated the operation; did it again; compared the insignificant whitewashed streak with the far-reaching continent of unwhitewashed fence, and sat down on a tree-box discouraged. Jim came skipping out at the gate with a tin pail, and singing "Buffalo Gals." Bringing water from the town pump had always been hateful work in Tom's eyes, before, but now it did not strike him so. He remembered that there was company at the pump. White, mulatto, and negro boys and girls were always there waiting their turns, resting, trading playthings, quarreling, fighting, skylarking. And he remembered that although the pump was only a hundred and fifty yards off, Jim never got back with a bucket of water under an hour—and even then somebody generally had to go after him. Tom said:

3   "Say, Jim, I'll fetch the water if you'll whitewash some."

4   Jim shook his head and said:

5   "Can't, Mars Tom. Ole missis, she tole me I got to go an' git dis water an' not stop foolin' roun' wid anybody. She say she spec' Mars Tom gwine to ax me to whitewash, an' so she tole me go 'long an' 'tend to my own business—she 'lowed *she'd* 'tend to de whitewashin'."

6   "Oh, never you mind what she said, Jim. That's the way she always talks. Gimme the bucket—I won't be gone only a minute. *She* won't ever know."

7   "Oh, I dasn't Mars Tom. Ole missis she'd take an' tar de head off'n me. 'Deed she would."

8   "*She!* She never licks anybody—whacks 'em over the head with her thimble—and who cares for that, I'd like to know. She talks awful, but talk don't hurt—anyways it don't if she don't cry. Jim, I'll give you a marvel. I'll give you a white alley!"

9   Jim began to waver.

10   "White alley, Jim! And it's a bully taw."

11   "My! Dat's a mighty gay marvel, *I* tell you! But Mars Tom I's powerful 'fraid ole missis—"

12   "And besides, if you will I'll show you my sore toe."

13   Jim was only human—this attraction was too much for him. He put down his pail, took the white alley, and bent over the toe with absorbing interest while the bandage was being unwound. In another moment he was flying down the street with his pail and a tingling rear, Tom was whitewashing with vigor, and Aunt Polly was retiring from the field with a slipper in her hand and triumph in her eye.

14   But Tom's energy did not last. He began to think of the fun he had planned for this day, and his sorrows multiplied. Soon the free boys would come tripping along on all sorts of delicious expeditions, and they would make a world of fun of him for having to work—the very thought of it burnt him like fire. He got out his worldly wealth and examined it—bits of toys, marbles, and trash; enough to buy an exchange of *work* maybe, but not half enough to buy so much as half an hour of pure freedom. So he returned his straightened means to his pocket, and gave up the idea of trying to buy the boys. At this dark and hopeless moment an inspiration burst upon him! Nothing less than a great, magnificent inspiration.

15   He took up his brush and went tranquilly to work. Ben Rogers hove in sight presently—the very boy, of all boys, whose ridicule he had been dreading. Ben's gait was the hop-skip-and-jump—proof enough that his heart was light and his anticipations high. He was eating an apple, and giving a long, melodious whoop, at intervals, followed by a deep-toned ding-dong-dong, ding-dong-dong, for he was personating a steamboat. As he drew near, he slackened speed, took the middle of the street, leaned far over to starboard and rounded to ponderously and with laborious pomp and circumstance—for he was personating the "Big Missouri," and considered himself to be drawing nine feet of water. He was boat, and captain, and engine-bells combined, so he had to imagine himself standing on his own hurricane-deck giving the orders and executing them:

16   "Stop her, sir! Ting-a-ling-ling!" The headway ran almost out and he drew up slowly toward the side-walk.

17   "Ship up to back! Ting-a-ling-ling!" His arms straightened and stiffened down his sides.

18   "Set her back on the stabboard! Ting-a-ling-ling! Chow! ch-chow-wow! Chow!" His right hand, meantime, describing stately circles—for it was representing a forty-foot wheel.

19   "Let her go back on the labboard! Ting-a-ling-ling! Chow-ch-chow-chow!" The left hand began to describe circles.

20   "Stop the stabboard! Ting-a-ling-ling! Stop the labboard! Come ahead on the stabboard! Stop her! Let your outside turn over slow! Ting-a-ling-ling! Chow-ow-ow! Get out that head-line! *Lively* now! Come—out with your spring-line—what're you about there! Take a turn round that stump with the bight of it! Stand by that stage,

now—let her go! Done with the engines, sir! Ting-a-ling-ling! *Sh't! sh't! sh't!*" (trying the gauge-cocks).

21   Tom went on whitewashing—paid no attention to the steamboat. Ben stared a moment and then said:

22   "Hi-*yi! You're* up a stump, ain't you!

23   No answer. Tom surveyed his last touch with the eye of an artist; then he gave his brush another gentle sweep and surveyed the result, as before. Ben ranged up alongside of him. Tom's mouth watered for the apple, but he stuck to his work. Ben said:

24   "Hello, old chap, you got to work, hey?"

25   Tom wheeled suddenly and said:

26   "Why it's you Ben! I warn't noticing."

27   "Say—*I'm* going in a swimming, *I* am. Don't you wish you could? But of course you'd druther *work*—wouldn't you? Course you would!"

28   Tom contemplated the boy a bit, and said:

29   "What do you call work?"

30   "Why ain't *that* work?"

31   Tom resumed his whitewashing, and answered carelessly:

32   "Well, maybe it is, and maybe it ain't. All I know, is, it suits Tom Sawyer."

33   "Oh come, now, you don't mean to let on that you *like* it?"

34   The brush continued to move.

35   "Like it? Well I don't see why I oughtn't to like it. Does a boy get a chance to whitewash a fence every day?"

36   That put the thing in a new light. Ben stopped nibbling his apple. Tom swept his brush daintily back and forth—stepped back to note the effect—added a touch here and there—criticised the effect again—Ben watching every move and getting more and more interested, more and more absorbed. Presently he said:

37   "Say, Tom, let *me* whitewash a little."

38   Tom considered, was about to consent; but he altered his mind:

39   "No—no—I reckon it wouldn't hardly do, Ben. You see, Aunt Polly's awful particular about this fence—right here on the street, you know—but if it was the back fence I wouldn't mind and *she* wouldn't. Yes, she's awful particular about this fence; it's got to be done very careful; I reckon there ain't one boy in a thousand, maybe two thousand, that can do it the way it's got to be done."

40   "No—is that so? Oh come, now—lemme just try. Only just a little—I'd let *you*, if you was me, Tom."

41   "Ben, I'd like to, honest injun; but Aunt Polly—well Jim wanted to do it, but she wouldn't let him; Sid wanted to do it, and she wouldn't let Sid. Now don't you see how I'm fixed? If you was to tackle this fence and anything was to happen to it—"

42   "Oh, shucks, I'll be just as careful. Now lemme try. Say—I'll, give you the core of my apple."

43   "Well, here—. No Ben, now don't. I'm afeard—"

44   "I'll give you *all* of it!"

45   Tom gave up the brush with reluctance in his face but alacrity in his heart. And while the late steamer "Big Missouri" worked and sweated in the sun, the retired artist sat on a barrel in the shade close by, dangled his legs, munched his apple, and planned the slaughter of more innocents. There was no lack of material; boys happened along every little while; they came to jeer, but remained to whitewash. By the time Ben was fagged out, Tom had traded the next chance to Billy Fisher for a kite, in good repair; and when *he* played out, Johnny Miller bought in for a dead rat and a string to swing it with—and so on, and so on, hour after hour. And when the middle of the afternoon came, from being a poor poverty-stricken boy in the morning, Tom was literally rolling in wealth. He had beside the things before mentioned, twelve marbles, part of a Jew's-harp, a piece of blue bottle-glass to look through, a spool cannon, a key that wouldn't unlock anything, a fragment of chalk, a stopper of a decanter, a tin soldier, a couple of tadpoles, six firecrackers, a kitten with only one eye, a brass door-knob, a dogcollar—but no dog—the handle of a knife, four pieces of orange peel, and a dilapidated old window-sash.

46   He had had a nice, good, idle time all the while—plenty of company—and the fence had three coats of whitewash on it! If he hadn't run out of whitewash, he would have bankrupted every boy in the village.

47   Tom said to himself that it was not such a hollow world, after all. He had discovered a great law of human action, without knowing it—namely, that in order to make a man or a boy covet a thing, it is only necessary to make the thing difficult to attain. If he had been a great and wise philosopher, like the writer of this book, he would now have comprehended that Work consists of whatever a body is *obliged* to do, and that Play consists of whatever a body is not obliged to do. And this would help him to understand why constructing artificial flowers or performing on a treadmill is work, while rolling ten-pins or climbing Mont Blanc is only amusement. There are wealthy gentlemen in England who drive four-horse passenger-coaches twenty or thirty miles on a daily line, in the summer, because the privilege costs them considerable money; but if they were offered wages for the service, that would turn it into work and then they would resign.

48   The boy mused a while over the substantial change which had taken place in his worldly circumstances, and then wended toward headquarters to report.

Strong Temptations—
Strategic Movements—
The Innocents Beguiled

JOURNAL

1. **MLA Works Cited**   *Using this model, record this story here.*

   Author's Last Name, First Name. "Title of the Story." *Title of the Book.* 2nd

   ed. Ed. First Name Last Name. City: Publisher, year. Page number(s) of

   this story. Print.

2. **Main Character(s)**   *Describe each main character, and explain why you think each is a main character.*

3. **Supporting Characters**   *Describe each supporting character, and explain why you think each is a supporting character.*

4. **Setting and Props**   *Describe the setting(s) and all relevant prop(s).*

5. **Sequence**   *Outline the events of the story in order.*

6. **Plot**   *Tell the story in no more than two sentences.*

7. **Conflicts**   *Identify and explain all the conflicts involved here.*

8. **Significant Quotations**   *Explain the importance of each of these quotations. Record the page number in the parentheses.*

   a. "He surveyed the fence, and all gladness left him [...]" (   ).

   b. "At this dark and hopeless moment an inspiration burst upon him! Nothing less than a great, magnificent inspiration" (   ).

   c. "Like it? Well I don't see why I oughtn't to like it. Does a boy get a chance to whitewash a fence every day?" (   ).

d. "Now don't you see how I'm fixed? If you was to tackle this fence and anything was to happen to it—"
"Oh, shucks, I'll be just as careful. Now lemme try. Say—I'll give you
the core of my apple [...]" (   ).

e. "And when the middle of the afternoon came, from being a poor poverty-
stricken boy in the morning, Tom was literally rolling in wealth" (   ).

9. **Literary Elements**   *Look at this chapter's title and explain why you think
this story is placed in this chapter. Explain in which other chapter(s) you
might place this story, as relevant to the literary element(s) of that chapter.*

10. **Foreshadowing, Irony, and/or Symbolism**   *Explain examples of foreshadowing, irony, and/or symbolism in this story.*

Follow-up Questions

10 Short Questions

What is the _best_ answer for each?

_____ 1. It is a
a. sunny day.
b. rainy day.
c. cold day.

_____ 2. Tom
a. does not paint the fence at all.
b. wants to paint the fence.
c. does not want to paint the fence.

_____ 3. Before, Tom had thought going to pump water was
a. a chore.
b. fun.
c. a good escape.

_____ 4. Now, Tom would rather
a. do chores.
b. paint the fence.
c. go to get water.

_____ 5. Ben seems to be
a. a stranger to Tom.
b. Tom's good friend.
c. Tom's rival.

_____ 6. Ben is
a. piloting a riverboat.
b. pretending to pilot a riverboat.
c. on a riverboat.

_____ 7. The boys consider riverboats to be
a. fun and adventuresome.
b. hard work.
c. boring and dull.

_____ 8. Tom tells Ben Aunt Polly is "'particular'"
a. to scare him away.
b. to insult him.
c. to lure him in.

_____ 9. Ben is
a. the only painter.
b. not the only painter.
c. the only other boy.

_____ 10. Tom
a. tricks the other boys into painting the fence.
b. does not trick the other boys into painting the fence.
c. cannot trick the other boys into painting the fence.

5 Significant Quotations

What is the importance of each of these quotations?

1. "Sighing he dipped his brush and passed it along the topmost plank; repeated the operation; did it again; compared the insignificant whitewashed streak with the far-reaching continent of unwhitewashed fence, and sat down on a tree-box discouraged."

2. "Bringing water from the town pump had always been hateful work in Tom's eyes, before, but now it did not strike him so."

3. "'Say, Tom, let _me_ whitewash a little.'"

4. "Tom gave up the brush with reluctance in his face but alacrity in his heart."

5. "There are wealthy gentlemen in England who drive four-horse passenger-coaches twenty or thirty miles on a daily line, in the summer, because the privilege costs them considerable money; but if they were offered wages for the service, that would turn it into work and then they would resign."

2 COMPREHENSION ESSAY QUESTIONS

Use specific details and information from the story to answer these questions as completely as possible.

1. The fence is central to this story. What is the significance of the fence? Use specific details and information from the story.

2. How does Tom trick the boys? Use specific details and information from the story to support your explanation.

DISCUSSION QUESTIONS

Be prepared to discuss these questions in class.

1. Do you think what Tom does is fair, smart, or unfair? Use specific details from the story to support your thinking.

2. When have you tricked someone? Using specific details from the story, compare and contrast your trickery with the tricks Tom plays.

WRITING

Use each of these ideas for writing an essay.

1. "Whitewashing" means to paint a surface with thin, white paint. "Whitewashing" has also come to mean covering up someone else's mess. Compare a time you used someone to cover up your mess or a time someone used you to cover up her or his mess to Tom's trickery.

2. "Whitewashing" also means to cover unpleasant facts with denials, lies, or half-truths. Tell the story of a time you or someone you know whitewashed facts.

Further Writing

1. Tom Sawyer in this story and Dee in "Everyday Use" by Alice Walker (available in a library) use ruses or pretenses to try to get what they want. Compare and contrast their manipulations and their goals.

2. Research the animal rights movement, and include a discussion of Twain's "A Dog's Tale" (available in a library), one of the most poignant and compelling pieces written that is germane to animal treatment.

CHAPTER 3

Plot and Foreshadowing

A story is based around a simple skeleton of events called a **plot**. Around this basic plot, a logical order of events or **sequence** occurs that builds tension or, in mysteries, suspense. In stories we call all the events in the sequence a **story line**.

Have you ever gone to the movies and watched the end credits roll while you were still waiting for the movie to get going? You looked at the person sitting next to you, felt cheated, and asked "What happened?" What happened is that, somewhere along the line, the storyteller failed.

In a well-written story, one event logically leads to another event, and then to another, and so on, so that each word and action counts and builds tension that carries your interest. The tension peaks at the **climax** and then resolves in the **dénouement**. When any one of these pieces is missing, poorly developed, or unbelievable, we are disappointed. (Movie sequels, in fact, purposely stop at the climax and before the dénouement so that we will return for the next episode.)

Each story in this chapter depends on the flow of events in the story. First, the narrator is caught up in events in "Bone Girl." Then Durante, who thinks he is in control of events, spins out of control in "Wine on the Desert." Finally, the one and only Edgar Allan Poe, the master of overwhelming atmospheres, draws us deeper and deeper into the events that swirl around the narrator in "The Tell-Tale Heart."

Foreshadowing is a technique some authors use to help explain or predict events to come. The author may sprinkle information or hints throughout the story to help predict actions that are yet to happen. Edgar Allan Poe is a master at foreshadowing. In his stories, there are hints along the way, although readers almost always miss the clues on the first reading and are astonished at the endings. See how well you can pick up these hints in "The Tell-Tale Heart." And pay special attention to the story-within-a-story that occurs in both "Bone Girl" and "Wine on the Desert." These stories offer classic examples of foreshadowing. After reading these stories in this chapter, look aback and notice that each has hints along the way that help predict the unsettling endings.

Bone Girl

JOSEPH BRUCHAC

PRE-READING VOCABULARY
CONTEXT

Use context clues to define these words before reading. Use a dictionary as needed.

1. The miners dug a big ditch into the ground that became the *quarry* where they would mine for ore. *Quarry* means _____.

2. The government set aside specific land for the Native Americans to settle on and build their town in this *reservation* or, as they called it, "the *res.*" *Reservation* or *res* means _____.

3. Little Mike is sometimes afraid of the ghosts or *spirits* and becomes scared on Halloween. *Spirit* means _____.

4. The murderer was *condemned* to spend the rest of his life in jail, alone, with no hope of freedom. *Condemned* means

    _____.

5. Native Americans are also referred to as *Indians*, a name that supposedly comes from Columbus's belief that he had found the water passage to India. *Indian* means _____.

6. When people die, they are normally taken to the *graveyard* or cemetery to be buried with others who have died. *Graveyard* means _____.

7. A particularly ugly or mean ghost may be referred to as a *ghoul*. *Ghoul* means _____.

8. Alice's *ancestors* came to America over two hundred years ago, and settled in New Jersey. *Ancestor* means _____.

9. Missy *dreaded* going to her boss's office because she was always afraid she would say the wrong thing. *Dread* means _____.

10. Michelle is very *familiar* with everyone in her family because she knows them all well and sees them often. *Familiar* means

_____.

11. Patrice is a real *neurotic* about her soap opera; she almost seems to think the characters are real. *Neurotic* means _____.

12. Allison has beautiful *blond* hair that is the color of pale yellow roses. *Blond* means _____.

13. In order to get across the river, John had to get in traffic and drive over the *bridge*. *Bridge* means _____.

14. Sarah was a very *shy* child who seemed afraid to speak to anyone, but now she talks to everyone. *Shy* means _____.

15. Tom thought he would create *romance* and invited his fiancée, Jacky, out for a candlelit dinner under the stars. *Romance* means

_____.

16. Jake is no *fool*; he studies carefully and is completely aware of all the people and events around him. *Fool* means _____.

17. Arjay loves *spooky* movies and enjoys reading ghost and horror stories. *Spooky* means _____.

18. A full *moon* lights the night sky with its reflection, even if it is hidden behind clouds. *Moon* means _____.

19. Laura has an exquisitely beautiful *face*; her eyes sparkle above her delicately shaped nose and bright smile. *Face* means

_____.

20. After the skin and muscles had rotted away, all that was left of the corpse's head was the *skull*. *Skull* means _____.

PRE-READING VOCABULARY
STRUCTURAL ATTACK

Define these words by solving the parts. Use the Glossary or a dictionary as needed.

1. outsiders
2. international
3. drainage
4. resurfaced
5. homeless
6. disconnected

7. development
8. flickering
9. goofing
10. staggering
11. old-fashioned
12. high-buttoned

PRE-READING QUESTIONS

Try answering these questions as you read.

Where does the narrator live?

How does the narrator feel about spirits?

What happens to the narrator?

Bone Girl

JOSEPH BRUCHAC

Joseph Bruchac is of Abenaki heritage. He shares his heritage in his many writings and in his role of the storyteller, a role and revered position that is absolutely essential to the transmission of culture within a tribe or community. He has told his stories around the world. Some of his other writings are *The Dawn Land* and *Turtle Meat.*

The Storyteller - Hopi Statuette

There is this one old abandoned quarry on the reservation where she is often seen. Always late, late at night when there is a full moon. The kind of moon that is as white as bone.

2   Are ghosts outsiders? That is the way most white people seem to view them. Spirits who are condemned to wander for eternity. Ectoplasmic remnants of people whose violent deaths left their spirits trapped between the worlds. You know what I mean. I'm sure. I bet we've seen the same movies and TV shows. Vengeful apparitions. Those are real popular. And then there is this one: scary noises in the background, the lights get dim, and a hushed voice saying "But what they didn't know was that the house had been built on an *Indian graveyard!*" And the soundtrack fills with muted tomtoms. Bum-bum-bum-bum, bum-bum-bum-bum.

3   Indian graveyards. White people seem to love to talk about them. They're this continent's equivalent of King Tut's tomb. On the one hand, I wish some white people in particular really were more afraid of them than they are—those people that some call "pot hunters," though I think the good old English word "ghoul" applies pretty well. There's a big international trade in Indian grave goods dug up and sold. And protecting them and getting back the bones of our ancestors who've been dug up and stolen and taken to museums, that is real important to us. I can tell you more about that, but that is another tale to tell another time. I'd better finish this story first.

4   Indian graveyards, you see, mean something different to me than places of dread. Maybe it's because I've spent a lot of time around real Indian graveyards, not the ones in the movies. Like the one the kids on our res walk by on their way to school—just like I used to. That cemetery is an old one, placed right in the middle of the town. It's a lot older than the oldest marker stones in it. In the old days, my people used to bury those who died right under the foundation of the lodge. No marker stones then. Just the house and your relatives continued to live there. That was record enough of the life you'd had. It was different from one part of the country to another, I know. Different Indian people have different ways of dealing with death. In a lot of places it still isn't regarded as the right thing to do to say the names of those who've died after their bodies have gone back into the earth. But, even with that, I don't think that Indian ghosts *are* outsiders. They're still with us and part of us. No farther away from us than the other side of a leaf that has fallen. I think Chief Cornplanter of the Seneca people said that. But he wasn't the only one to say it. Indian ghosts are, well, familiar. Family. And when you're family, you care for each other. In a lot of different ways.

5   Being in my sixties, now, it gives me the right to say a few things. I want to say them better, which is why I have taken this extension course in creative writing. Why I have read the books assigned for this class. But when I put my name on something I have written, when you see the name Russell Painter on it, I would like it to be something I am proud of. I worked building roads for a good many years and I was always proud that I could lay out a road just so. The crest was right and the shoulders were right and that road was even and the turns banked and the drainage good so that ice didn't build up. Roads eventually wear away and have to be resurfaced and all that, but if you make a road right then you can use it to get somewhere. So I would like to write in the same way. I would like any story I tell to get somewhere and not be a dead end or so poorly made that it is full of holes and maybe even throws someone off it into the ditch. This is called an extended metaphor.

6   You may note that I am not writing in the style which I have begun to call "cute Indian." There is this one Canadian who pretends to be an Indian when he writes and his Indians are very cute and he has a narrator telling his stories who is doing what I am doing, taking a creative writing course. My writing instructor is a good enough guy. My writing instructor would like me to get cuter. That is why he has had me read some books that can furnish me, as he put it, with some good "boilerplate models." But I think I have enough models just by looking at the people around me and trying to understand the lessons they've taught me. Like I said, as I said, being in my sixties and retired gives me the right to say some things. Not that I didn't have the right to say them before. Just that now I may actually be listened to when I start talking.

7   Like about Indian ghosts. Most of the real ghost stories I have heard from people in the towns around the res don't seem to have a point to them. It's always someone hearing a strange noise or seeing a light or the furniture moving or windows shutting or strange shapes walking down a hallway. Then they may find out later that someone died in that house a long time ago and that the spirit of that person is probably what has been making those weird things happen. Our ghost stories make sense. Or maybe it is more like our ghosts have a sense of purpose. I have a theory about this. I think it is because Indians stay put and white people keep moving around. White people bury their dead in a graveyard full of people they don't know and then they move away themselves. Get a better job in a city on the West Coast or maybe retire to Florida. And those ghosts—even if they've stayed in the family home—they're surrounded by strangers. I think maybe those ghosts get to be like the homeless people you see wandering around the streets in the big cities these days. Talking to themselves, ignored unless they really get into your face, disconnected and forgotten.

8   But Indian people stay put—unless they're forced to move. Like the Cherokees being forced out of the south or the way the Abenakis were driven out of western Maine or the Stockbridge people or, to be honest, just about every Indian nation you can name at one time or another. There's still a lot of forcing Indian people to move going on today. I could tell you some stories about our own res. Last year they were planning to put in a big housing development that would have taken a lot of land up on Turkey Hill. That little mountain isn't officially ours anymore, but we hope to get it back one day. And that development would have polluted our water, cut down a lot of trees we care about. Maybe someday I will write a story about how that housing development got stalled and then this "recession-depression" came along and knocked the bottom out

of the housing market. So that development went down the tubes. But some folks I know were involved in stopping that development, and they might get in trouble if I told you what they did. And I am digressing, my writing instructor is probably writing in the margin of this story right now. Except he doesn't understand that is how we tell stories. In circles. Circling back to the fact that Indian people like to stay put. And because we stay put, close to the land where we were born (and even though my one-story house may not look like much, I'm the fifth generation of Painters to live in it and it stands on the same earth where a log cabin housed four generations before that and a bark lodge was there when the Puritans were trying to find a stone to stand on), we also stay close to the land where we're buried. Close to our dead. Close to our ghosts—which, I assume, do not feel as abandoned as white ghosts and so tend to be a lot less neurotic. We know them, they know us, and they also know what they can do. Which often is, pardon my French, to scare the shit out of us when we're doing the wrong things!

9   I've got a nephew named Tommy. Typical junior high. He's been staying with my wife and me the last six months. Him and some of the other kids his age decided to have some fun and so they went one night and hid in the graveyard near the road, behind some of the bigger stones there. They had a piece of white cloth tied onto a stick and a lantern. They waited till they saw people walking home past the graveyard and as soon as they were close they made spooky noises and waved that white cloth and flashed the light. Just about everybody took off! I guess they'd never seen some of those older folks move that fast before! The only one they didn't scare was Grama Big Eel. She just paid no attention to it at all and just kept on walking. She didn't even turn her head.

10   Next night Tommy was walking home by himself, right past the same graveyard. As soon as he hit that spot a light started flickering in the graveyard and he could see something white.

11   "Okay, you guys!" he said. "I know you're there. You're not scaring me!" He kept right on going, trying not to speed up too much. He knew it was them, but he also wondered how come the light was a different color tonight and how they were able to make it move so fast through that graveyard.

12   As soon as he got home, the phone rang. It was one of his friends who'd been with him in the graveyard the night before, scaring people.

13   "Thought you scared me, didn't you?" Tommy said.

14   "Huh?" his friend answered. "I don't know what you mean. The guys are all here. They've been here the last two hours playing Nintendo. We were just wondering if you wanted to go back down to the graveyard again tonight and spook people."

15   After that, you can bet that Tommy stopped goofing around in the graveyard.

16   There's a lot more stories like that one. The best stories we can tell, though, are always the stories where the jokes are on ourselves. Which brings me to the story I wanted to tell when I started writing this piece.

17   When I came back home, retired here, I came back alone. My wife and I had some problems and we split up. There were some things I did here that weren't too bad, but I was drinking too much. And when they say there's no fool like an old fool, I guess I ought to know who they was talking about. I'd always liked the young girls too. Especially those ones with the blond hair. Right now if there's any Indian women reading this I bet they are about ready to give up in disgust. They know the type. That was me. Oh honey, sweetie, wait up for Grampa Russell. Lemme buy you another beer, lemme just give you a little hug, honey, sweetie. People were getting pretty disgusted with me. Nobody said anything. That would have been interfering. But when they saw me sleeping it off next to the road with a bottle in my hand, they must have been shaking their heads. I've always been real tough and even now I like to sleep outside, even when it gets cold. I have got me a bed in the field behind our house. But I wasn't sleeping in no bed in those days. I was sleeping in the ditches. Tommy wasn't living with me then or he would have been really ashamed of his Uncle Russell.

18   One Saturday night, I was coming home real, real late. There's a little bridge that is down about a mile from my house on one of the

little winding back roads that makes its way up to the big highway that cuts through the res. I had been at one of those bars they built just a hundred yards past the line. I'd stayed out even later than the younger guys who had the car and so I was walking home. Staggering, more like. The moonlight was good and bright, though, so it was easy to make my way and I was singing something in Indian as I went. That little bridge was ahead of me and I saw her there on the bridge. It was a young woman with long pale hair. Her face was turned away from me. She was wearing a long dress and it showed off her figure real good. She looked like she was maybe in her twenties from her figure and the way she moved. I couldn't see her face. I knew there was some girls visiting from the Cherokees and figured maybe she was one of them. Some of those southern Indian girls have got that long blond hair and you can't tell they're Indian till you see it in their face or the way they carry themselves. And from the way she moved she was sure Indian. And she was out looking for something to do late at night.

19   "Hey, honey!" I yelled. "Hey, sweetie, wait for me. Wait up."

20   She paused there on the bridge and let me catch up to her. I came up real close.

21   "Hi, sweetie," I said. "Is it okay if I walk with you some?"

22   She didn't say anything, just kept her head turned away from me. I like that. I've always liked the shy ones...or at least the ones who pretend to be shy to keep you interested. I put my arm around her shoulders and she didn't take it off; she just kept walking and I walked with her. I kept talking, saying the kind of no sense things that an old fool says when he's trying to romance a young girl. We kept on walking and next thing I knew we were at the old quarry. That was okay by me. There was a place near the road where there's a kind of natural seat in the stones and that's right where she led me and we sat down together.

23   Oh, was that moon bright! It glistened on her hair and I kept my left arm tight around her. She felt awfully cold and I figured she wouldn't mind my helping her get warm. I still had the bottle in my right hand and I figured that would get her to turn her head and look at me. I still hadn't seen her face under that long pale hair of hers.

24   "Come on, honey, you want a drink, huh?" But it didn't work. She kept her face turned away. So I decided that a drink wasn't what she wanted at all. "Sweetie," I said, "why don't you turn around and give old Grampa Russell a little kiss?"

25   And she turned her head.

26   They say the first time she was seen on the reservation was about two hundred years ago. She was dressed then the way she was that

night. Her hair loose and long, wearing an old-fashioned long dress and wearing those tall high-button shoes. I should have recognized those shoes. But no one ever does when they go to that quarry with her. They never recognize who she is until she turns her face to look at them. That skull face of hers that is all bone. Pale and white as the moon.

27   I dropped the bottle and let go of her. I ran without looking back and I'm pretty sure that she didn't follow me. I ran and I ran and even in my sleep I was still running when I woke up the next morning on the floor inside the house. That day I went and talked to some people and they told me what I had to do if I didn't want the Bone Girl to come and visit me.

28   That was two years ago and I haven't had a drink since then and with Mary and me having gotten back together and with Tommy living with us, I don't think I'll ever go back to those ways again.

29   So that is about all I have to say in this story, about ghosts and all. About Indian ghosts in particular and why it is that I say that Indian ghosts aren't outsiders. They're what you might call familiar spirits.

Bone Girl

JOURNAL

1. **MLA Works Cited**   *Using this model, record this story here.*

   Author's Last Name, First Name. "Title of the Story." *Title of the Book.*

       2nd ed. Ed. First Name Last Name. City: Publisher, year. Page number(s) of

       this story. Print.

2. **Main Character(s)**   *Describe each main character, and explain why you think each is a main character.*

3. **Supporting Characters**   *Describe each supporting character, and explain why you think each is a supporting character.*

4. **Setting and Props**   *Describe the setting(s) and all relevant prop(s).*

5. Sequence   *Outline the events of the story in order.*

6. Plot   *Tell the story in no more than two sentences.*

7. Conflicts   *Identify and explain all the conflicts involved here.*

8. Significant Quotations   *Explain the importance of each of these quotations. Record the page number in the parentheses.*

   a. "But, even with that, I don't think that Indian ghosts *are* outsiders" (   ).

   b. "I think it is because Indians stay put and white people keep moving around" (   ).

c. "'Huh?' his friend answered. 'I don't know what you mean. The guys are all here'" (   ).

d. "'Come on, honey, you want a drink, huh?'" (   ).

e. "I dropped the bottle and let go of her" (   ).

9. **Literary Elements**   *Look at this chapter's title and explain why you think this story is placed in this chapter. Explain in which other chapter(s) you might place this story, as relevant to the literary element(s) of that chapter.*

10. **Foreshadowing, Irony, and/or Symbolism**   *Explain examples of foreshadowing, irony, and/or symbolism in this story.*

Follow-up Questions

10 Short Questions

What is the _best_ answer for each?

_____ 1. The narrator's heritage is
a. white.
b. Native American.
c. other.

_____ 2. The narrator is
a. married.
b. single.
c. divorced.

_____ 3. The narrator believes that Native spirits are
a. all warlike or hurtful.
b. scary.
c. an extension of life.

_____ 4. The narrator believes that Native spirits are
a. similar to Western spirits.
b. different from Western spirits.
c. irrelevant to the living.

_____ 5. The narrator's nephew
a. tries to scare people.
b. scares everyone.
c. does not believe in spirits.

_____ 6. The narrator's nephew seems to
a. become a ghost.
b. run into a ghost.
c. be scared by his friends.

_____ 7. The narrator is writing about this story
a. to clear his conscience.
b. to be a "cute Indian."
c. for a writing course.

_____ 8. The narrator has
a. always been happily married.
b. never been married.
c. some marital problems.

_____ 9. At first, the narrator does not think the Bone Girl is
a. an available young girl.
b. chilly from the weather.
c. a spirit.

_____ 10. After meeting with the Bone Girl, the narrator
a. mends his life.
b. continues his drinking and debauchery.
c. dies.

5 Significant Quotations

What is the importance of each of these quotations?

1. "They're still with us and part of us. No farther away from us than the other side of a leaf that has fallen."

2. "I think it is because Indians stay put and white people keep moving around."

3. "He knew it was them, but he also wondered how come the light was a different color tonight and how they were able to make it move so fast through that graveyard."

4. "I still hadn't seen her face under that long pale hair of hers."

5. "That was two years ago […]."

2 COMPREHENSION ESSAY QUESTIONS

Use specific details and information from the story to answer these questions as completely as possible.

1. How is the narrator's idea of staying "put" significant to this story? Use specific details and information from the story to support your answer.

2. How is the title relevant to the story? Use specific details and information from the story to support your answer.

DISCUSSION QUESTIONS

Be prepared to discuss these questions in class.

1. Would you describe the Bone Girl as helpful or frightful?

2. What do you believe about spirits, and how does your thinking compare with the narrator's thinking?

WRITING

Use each of these ideas for writing an essay.

1. The narrator tells us, "I have a theory about this. I think it is because Indians stay put and white people keep moving around" (page 103). Thinking of your own family or community, write an essay that refutes or substantiates the narrator's thinking.

2. The encounter with the Bone Girl helps the narrator to straighten out his life. Many of us have had, or know of someone who has had, the experience of a supernatural intervention. Write about a supernatural intervention you know about and explain the effects this has had on the person involved.

Further Writing

1. The narrator refers to his excessive drinking. Research the effects alcohol has had on Native American communities.

2. The Bone Girl seems to be a rather benevolent spirit. Compare and contrast her with the spirit in Edgar Allan Poe's "The Masque of the Red Death" (available in a library).

Wine on the Desert

MAX BRAND

PRE-READING VOCABULARY
CONTEXT

Use context clues to define these words before reading. Use a dictionary as needed.

1. Alice occasionally enjoys a glass of white *wine* made from the grapes grown in Napa Valley. *Wine* means _____.

2. When Angela went to Arizona, all the sand and hot weather reminded her of the *Desert*. Desert means _____.

3. When Heather wanted to enforce the law, she became a county *sheriff* to investigate crimes and uphold the law. *Sheriff* means

   _____.

4. Anna joined a *posse* of people to help Sheriff Heather investigate and pursue criminals. *Posse* means _____.

5. Debbie became interested in wines and decided to buy a *vineyard* so that she could grow her own grapes. *Vineyard* means

   _____.

6. Dan bought several large metal *tanks* to hold water for the sprinkling system in his yard. *Tank* means _____.

7. When it did not rain for days and days, Gert had to water her plants during the *drought*. *Drought* means _____.

8. After running the mile and sweating a lot, Joseph was very dry and *thirsty* and just wanted a drink of water. *Thirsty* means

   _____.

9. In order to get a drink of water out of the large open container on the ranch, Anthony used a ladle or *dipper*. *Dipper* means

_____.

10. To go duck hunting, Wilson bought a long *Winchester rifle* that took large bullets and was three feet long. *Winchester rifle* means

_____.

11. In order to learn how to use a gun, Sallie bought a small *Colt revolver* and went to practice at a firing range. *Colt revolver* means

_____.

12. Santi found the water in the tub had *leaked* out through a large hole in the bottom of the tub. *Leak* means _____.

13. When he went camping, Patrick took a small *canteen* filled with water that he carried in his backpack. *Canteen* means

_____.

14. To carry the new gun that she was given by the sheriff, Georgiana bought a *holster* that she belted around her waist. *Holster* means

_____.

15. Jennifer is very afraid of loud thunder and lives in *terror* of a thunderstorm coming when she is alone. *Terror* means

_____.

16. After Zachary was woken up too early, he *staggered* back and forth around the room until he woke up. *Stagger* means

_____.

17. When Mark lost his wallet and could not remember where anything was, he thought he was losing his mind and going *mad*. *Mad* means

_____.

18. When Lucille has lunch, she eats very slowly and is always careful to *swallow* her food slowly. *Swallow* means _____.

19. When Carl ate his dinner too fast, he swallowed too fast and nearly *choked* on a piece of meat. *Choke* means _____.

20. MaryBeth loves the *still* of the night when everything is so quiet and she can hear a single drop of rain. *Still* means _____.

PRE-READING VOCABULARY
STRUCTURAL ATTACK

Define these words by solving the parts. Use a dictionary as needed.

1. dryness
2. windmill
3. accounted
4. darkened
5. unstirred
6. reddish
7. powdered
8. flowering
9. sweetness
10. coolness
11. wooden
12. stiffness
13. sunset
14. loosening
15. fifteen-shot
16. semicircle
17. dogtrot
18. useless
19. heartily
20. uncorked
21. lukewarm
22. horribly
23. thundering

PRE-READING QUESTIONS

Try answering these questions as you read.

Who is Durante?

Who is Tony?

Where are they?

What happens to Tony's father? Tony? Durante?

Wine on the Desert

MAX BRAND

Max Brand was born Frederick Shiller Faust in Seattle in 1892. He developed his love of reading from his mother, who died when he was only eight. After his father died five years later, Faust lived with different relatives until he attended the University of California at Berkeley. Creativity and self-defeat began to emerge as themes in Faust's life. At Berkeley, he became a literary star but failed to receive his degree due to his own vitriolic radicalism. He wanted to become an esteemed epic poet, but instead he made a fortune as a narrative Western, detective story, and screenplay writer. He wanted to join the World War I effort but deserted. He joined the World War II effort as a war correspondent but was killed on the first day of hostilities at Santa Maria Infante.

Faust was a prolific writer, writing an estimated 30 million words under various pen names. His most renowned works are *Destry Rides Again, Singing Guns,* and the *Dr. Kildare* series. His other works appear in many collections. His works can be found in libraries and in video stores.

There was no hurry, except for the thirst, like clotted salt, in the back of his throat, and Durante rode on slowly, rather enjoying the last moments of dryness before he reached the cold water in Tony's house. There was really no hurry at all. He had almost twenty-four hours' head start, for they would not find his dead man until this morning. After that, there would be perhaps several hours of delay before the sheriff gathered a sufficient posse and started on his trail. Or perhaps the sheriff would be fool enough to come alone.

2 Durante had been able to see the wheel and fan of Tony's windmill for more than an hour, but he could not make out the ten acres of the vineyard until he had topped the last rise, for the vines had been planted in a hollow. The lowness of the ground, Tony used to say, accounted for the water that gathered in the well during the wet season. The rains sank through the desert sand, through the gravels beneath, and gathered in a bowl of clay hardpan far below. In the middle of the rainless season the well ran dry, but long before that, Tony had every drop of the water pumped up into a score of tanks made of cheap corrugated iron. Slender pipe lines carried the water from the tanks to the vines and from time to time let them sip enough life to keep them until the winter darkened overhead suddenly, one November day, and the rain came down, and all the earth made a great hushing sound as it drank. Durante had heard that whisper of drinking when he was here before, but he never had seen the place in the middle of the long drought.

3 The windmill looked like a sacred emblem to Durante, and the twenty stodgy, tar-painted tanks blessed his eyes; but a heavy sweat broke out at once from his body. For the air of the hollow, unstirred by wind, was hot and still as a bowl of soup—a reddish soup. The vines were powdered with thin red dust also. They were wretched, dying things to look at, for the grapes had been gathered, the new wine had been made, and now the leaves hung in ragged tatters.

4 Durante rode up to the squat adobe house and right through the entrance into the patio. A flowering vine clothed three sides of the little court. Durante did not know the name of the plant, but it had large white blossoms with golden hearts that poured sweetness on the air. Durante hated the sweetness. It made him more thirsty.

5 He threw the reins of his mule and strode into the house. The water cooler stood in the hall outside the kitchen. There were two jars made of a porous stone, very ancient things, and the liquid which distilled through the pores kept the contents cool. The jar on the left held water; that on the right contained wine. There was a big tin dipper hanging on a peg beside each jar. Durante tossed off the cover of the vase on the left and plunged it in until the delicious coolness closed well above his wrist.

6   "Hey, Tony," he called. Out of his dusty throat the cry was a mere groaning. He drank and called again, clearly, "Tony!"

7   A voice pealed from the distance.

8   Durante, pouring down the second dipper of water, smelled the alkali dust which had shaken off his own clothes. It seemed to him that heat was radiating like light from his clothes, from his body, and the cool dimness of the house was soaking it up. He heard the wooden leg of Tony bumping on the ground, and Durante grinned. Then Tony came in with that hitch and side swing with which he accommodated the stiffness of his artificial leg. His brown face shone with sweat as though a special ray of light were focused on it.

9   "Ah, Dick!" he said. "Good old Dick! How long since you came last! Wouldn't Julia be glad! Wouldn't she be glad!"

10   "Ain't she here?" asked Durante, jerking his head suddenly away from the dripping dipper.

11   "She's away at Nogales," said Tony. "It gets so hot. I said, 'You go up to Nogales, Julia, where the wind don't forget to blow.' She cried, but I made her go."

12   "Did she cry?" asked Durante.

13   "Julia...that's a good girl," said Tony.

14   "Yeah. You wouldn't throw some water into that mule of mine, would you, Tony?"

15   Tony went out, with his wooden leg clumping loud on the wooden floor, softly in the patio dust. Durante found the hammock in the corner of the patio. He lay down in it and watched the color of sunset flush the mists of desert dust that rose to the zenith. The water was soaking through his body. Hunger began, and then the rattling of pans in the kitchen and the cheerful cry of Tony's voice:

16   "What you want, Dick? I got some pork. You don't want pork? I'll make you some good Mexican beans. Hot. I have plenty of good wine for you, Dick. Tortillas. Even Julia can't make tortillas like me. And what about a nice young rabbit?"

17   "All blowed full of buckshot?" growled Durante.

18   "No, no. I kill them with the rifle."

19   "You kill rabbits with a rifle?" repeated Durante, with a quick interest.

20   "It's the only gun I have," said Tony. "If I catch them in the sights, they are dead. A wooden leg cannot walk very far. I must kill them quick. You see? They come close to the house about sunrise and flop their ears. I shoot through the head."

21   "Yeah? Yeah?" muttered Durante. "Through the head?" He relaxed, scowling. He passed his hand over his face, over his head.

22   Then Tony began to bring the food out into the patio and lay it on a small wooden table. A lantern hanging against the wall of the house included the table in a dim half-circle of light. They sat there and ate. Tony had scrubbed himself for the meal. His hair was soaked in water and sleeked back over his round skull. A man in the desert might be willing to pay five dollars for as much water as went to the soaking of that hair.

23   Everything was good. Tony knew how to cook, and he knew how to keep the glasses filled with wine.

24   "This is old wine. This is my father's wine. Eleven years old," said Tony. "You look at the light through it. You see that brown in the red? That's the soft that time puts in good wine, my father always said."

25   "What killed your father?" asked Durante.

26   Tony lifted his hand as though he were listening or as though he were pointing out a thought.

27   "The desert killed him. I found his mule. It was dead, too. There was a leak in the canteen. My father was only five miles away when the buzzards showed him to me."

28   "Five miles? Just an hour...Good Lord!" said Durante. He stared with big eyes. "Just dropped down and died?" he asked.

29   "No," said Tony. "When you die of thirst, you always die just one way. First you tear off your shirt, then your undershirt. That's to be cooler....And the sun comes and cooks your bare skin. And then you think...there is water everywhere, if you dig down far enough. You begin to dig. The dust comes up your nose. You start screaming. You break your nails in the sand. You wear the flesh off the tips of your fingers, to the bone." He took a quick swallow of wine.

30   "Unless you seen a man die of thirst, how d'you know they start screaming?" asked Durante.

31   "They got a screaming look when you find them," said Tony. "Take some more wine. The desert never can get to you here. My father showed me the way to keep the desert away from the hollow. We live pretty good here. No?"

32   "Yeah," said Durante, loosening his shirt collar. "Yeah, pretty good."

33   Afterward he slept well in the hammock until the report of a rifle waked him and he saw the color of dawn in the sky. It was such a great, round bowl that for a moment he felt as though he were above, looking down into it.

34   He got up and saw Tony coming in holding a rabbit by the ears, the rifle in his other hand.

35   "You see?" said Tony. "Breakfast came and called on us!" He laughed.

36   Durante examined the rabbit with care. It was nice and fat and it had been shot through the head—through the middle of the head. Such a shudder went down the back of Durante that he washed gingerly before breakfast. He felt that his blood was cooled for the entire day.

37   It was a good breakfast, too, with flapjacks and stewed rabbit with green peppers, and a quart of strong coffee. Before they had finished, the sun struck through the east window and started them sweating.

38   "Gimme a look at that rifle of yours, Tony, will you?" Durante asked.

39   "You take a look at my rifle, but don't you steal the luck that's in it," laughed Tony. He brought the fifteen-shot Winchester.

40   "Loaded right to the brim?" asked Durante.

41   "I always load it full the minute I get back home," said Tony.

42   "Tony, come outside with me," commanded Durante.

43   They went out from the house. The sun turned the sweat of Durante to hot water and then dried his skin so that his clothes felt transparent. "Tony, I gotta be mean," said Durante. "Stand right there where I can see you. Don't try to get close. Now listen. The sheriff's gunna be along this trail sometime today, looking for me. He'll load up himself and all his gang with water out of your tanks. Then he'll follow my sign across the desert. Get me? He'll follow if he finds water on the place. But he's not gunna find water."

44   "What you done, poor Dick?" said Tony. "Now look, I could hide you in the old wine cellar where nobody—"

45   "The sheriff's not gunna find water," said Durante. "It's gunna be like this."

46   He put the rifle to his shoulder, aimed, fired. The shot struck the base of the nearest tank, ranging down through the bottom. A semicircle of darkness began to stain the soil near the edge of the iron wall.

47   Tony fell on his knees. "No, no, Dick! Good Dick!" he said. "Look! All the vineyard. It will die. It will turn into old, dead wood, Dick..."

48   "Shut your face," said Durante. "Now I've started, I kinda like the job."

49   Tony fell on his face and put his hands over his ears. Durante drilled a bullet hole through the tanks, one after another. Afterward, he leaned on the rifle.

50   "Take my canteen and go in and fill it with water out of the cooling jar," he said, "Snap to it, Tony!"

51   Tony got up. He raised the canteen and looked around him, not at the tanks from which the water was pouring so that the noise of the earth drinking was audible, but at the rows of his vineyard. Then he went into the house.

52   Durante mounted his mule. He shifted the rifle to his left hand and drew out the heavy Colt from its holster. Tony came dragging back to him, his head down. Durante watched Tony with a careful revolver, but he gave up the canteen without lifting his eyes.

53   "The trouble with you, Tony," said Durante, "is you're yellow. I'd of fought a tribe of wildcats with my bare hands before I'd let 'em do what I'm doin' to you. But you sit back and take it."

54   Tony did not seem to hear. He stretched out his hands to the vines. "Will you let them all die?" he asked.

55   Durante shrugged his shoulders. He shook the canteen to make sure that it was full. It was so brimming that there was hardly room for the liquid to make a sloshing sound. Then he turned the mule and kicked it into a dogtrot. Half a mile from the house of Tony, he threw the empty rifle to the ground. There was no sense packing that useless weight, and Tony with his peg leg would hardly come this far.

56   Durante looked back, a mile or so later, and saw the little image of Tony picking up the rifle from the dust, then staring earnestly after his guest. Durante remembered the neat little hole clipped through the head of the rabbit. Wherever he went, his trail never could return again to the vineyard in the desert. But then, commencing to picture to himself the arrival of the sweating sheriff and his posse at the house of Tony, Durante laughed heartily.

57   The sheriff's posse could get plenty of wine, of course, but without water a man could not hope to make the desert voyage, even with a mule or a horse to help him on the way. Durante patted the full, rounding side of his canteen. He might even now begin with the first sip but it was a luxury to postpone pleasure until desire became greater.

58   He raised his eyes along the trail. Close by, it was merely dotted with occasional bones. But distance joined the dots into an unbroken chalk line which wavered with a strange leisure across the Apache Desert, pointing toward the cool blue promise of the mountains. The next morning he would be among them.

59   A coyote whisked out of a gully and ran like a gray puff of dust on the wind. His tongue hung out like a little red rag from the side of his mouth, and suddenly Durante was dry to the marrow. He uncorked and lifted his canteen. It had a slightly sour smell; perhaps the sacking which covered it had grown a trifle old. And then he poured a great mouthful of lukewarm liquid. He had swallowed it before his senses could give him warning.

60   It was wine!

61   He looked first of all toward the mountains. They were as calmly blue, as distant as when he had started that morning. Twenty-four hours not on water, but on wine!

62   "I deserve it," said Durante. "I trusted him to fill the canteen. I deserve it. Curse him!" With a mighty resolution, he quieted the panic in his soul. He would not touch the stuff until noon. Then he would take one discreet sip. He would win through.

63   Hours went by. He looked at his watch and found it was only ten o'clock. And he had thought that it was on the verge of noon! He uncorked the wine and drank freely and, corking the canteen, felt almost as though he needed a drink of water more than before. He sloshed the contents of the canteen. Already it was horribly light.

64   Once, he turned the mule and considered the return trip. But he could remember the head of the rabbit too clearly, drilled right through the center. The vineyard, the rows of old twisted, gnarled little trunks with the bark peeling off…every vine was to Tony like a human life. And Durante had condemned them all to death!

65   He faced the blue of the mountains again. His heart raced in his breast with terror. Perhaps it was fear and not the suction of that dry and deadly air that made his tongue cleave to the roof of his mouth.

66   The day grew old. Nausea began to work in his stomach, nausea alternating with sharp pains. When he looked down, he saw that there was blood on his boots. He had been spurring the mule until the red ran down from its flanks. It went with a curious stagger, like a rocking horse with a broken rocker. Durante grew aware that he had been keeping the mule at a gallop for a long time. He pulled it to a halt. It stood with wide-braced legs. Its head was down. When he leaned from the saddle, he saw that its mouth was open.

67   "It's gunna die," said Durante. "It's gunna die.…What a fool I been.…"

68   The mule did not die until after sunset. Durante left everything except his revolver. He packed the weight of that for an hour and discarded it, in turn. His knees were growing weak. When he looked up at the stars, they shone white and clear for a moment only, and then whirled into little racing circles and scrawls of red.

69   He lay down. He kept his eyes closed and waited for the shaking to go out of his body, but it would not stop. And every breath of darkness was like an inhalation of black dust. He got up and went on, staggering. Sometimes he found himself running.

70   Before you die of thirst, you go mad. He kept remembering that. His tongue had swollen big. Before it choked him, if he lanced it with his knife the blood would help him; he would be able to swallow. Then he remembered that the taste of blood is salty.

71   Once, in his boyhood, he had ridden through a pass with his father and they had looked down on the sapphire of a mountain lake, a hundred thousand million tons of water as cold as snow.…

72   When he looked up, now, there were no stars; and this frightened him terribly. He never had seen a desert night so dark. His eyes were failing; he was being blinded. When the morning came, he would not be able to see the mountains, and he would walk around and around in a circle until he dropped and died.

73   No stars, no wind; the air as still as the water of a stale pool, and he in the dregs at the bottom....

74   He seized his shirt at the throat and tore it away so that it hung in two rags from his hips.

75   He could see the earth only well enough to stumble on the rocks. But there were no stars in the heavens. He was blind. He had no more hope than a rat in a well. Ah, but devils know how to put poison in wine that will steal all the senses or any one of them. And Tony had chosen to blind Durante.

76   He heard a sound like water. It was the swishing of the soft, deep sand through which he was treading—sand so soft that a man could dig it away with his bare hands....

77   Afterward, after many hours, out of the blind face of that sky the rain began to fall. It made first a whispering and then a delicate murmur like voices conversing, but after that, just at the dawn, it roared like the hoofs of ten thousand charging horses. Even through that thundering confusion the big birds with naked heads and red, raw necks found their way down to one place in the Apache Desert.

Wine on the Desert

JOURNAL

1. **MLA Works Cited**   *Using this model, record this story here.*

   Author's Last Name, First Name. "Title of the Story." *Title of the Book.*

   2nd ed. Ed. First Name Last Name. City: Publisher, year. Page number(s)

   of this story. Print.

2. **Main Character(s)**   *Describe each main character, and explain why you think each is a main character.*

3. **Supporting Characters**   *Describe each supporting character, and explain why you think each is a supporting character.*

4. **Setting and Props**   *Describe the setting(s) and all relevant prop(s).*

5. **Sequence**   *Outline the events of the story in order.*

6. **Plot**   *Tell the story in no more than two sentences.*

7. **Conflicts**   *Identify and explain all the conflicts involved here.*

8. **Significant Quotations**   *Explain the importance of each of these quotations. Record the page number in the parentheses.*

   a. "He had almost twenty-four hours' head start, for they would not find his dead man until this morning" (   ).

   b. "In the middle of the rainless season the well ran dry, but long before that, Tony had every drop of the water pumped up into a score of tanks made of cheap corrugated iron" (   ).

c. "A man in the desert might be willing to pay five dollars for as much water as went to the soaking of that hair" (   ).

d. "Durante drilled a bullet hole through the tanks, one after another" (   ).

e. "He heard a sound like water. It was the swishing of the soft, deep sand through which he was treading—[...]" (   ).

9. **Literary Elements**   *Look at this chapter's title and explain why you think this story is placed in this chapter. Explain in which other chapter(s) you might place this story, as relevant to the literary element(s) of that chapter.*

10. **Foreshadowing, Irony, and/or Symbolism**   *Explain examples of foreshadowing, irony, and/or symbolism in this story.*

Follow-up Questions

10 Short Questions

What is the __best__ answer for each?

_____ 1. Durante probably has
   a. seen a man killed.
   b. killed a man.
   c. saved a man.

_____ 2. Durante is wanted by
   a. the sheriff.
   b. Julia.
   c. Tony.

_____ 3. Tony needs the tanks
   a. to store water.
   b. to store wine.
   c. to cool the windmill.

_____ 4. Tony needs the water
   a. to water the vineyard.
   b. to survive.
   c. both a and b

_____ 5. The story of Tony's father
   a. sets up the steps in dying from thirst.
   b. proves one can survive without water.
   c. is irrelevant to the story.

_____ 6. Tony and Durante
   a. are joined by Julia.
   b. are alone.
   c. are longtime enemies.

_____ 7. At Tony's house, Durante
   a. saves water.
   b. does not use water.
   c. wastes water.

_____ 8. For filling Durante's canteen, Tony
   a. gives Durante enough water.
   b. gives Durante wine.
   c. lets Durante fill the canteen.

_____ 9. After the canteen is filled,
   a. Durante takes off into the desert.
   b. Tony takes off into the desert.
   c. the sheriff arrests Durante.

_____ 10. In the end,
   a. Durante is arrested.
   b. Tony is arrested.
   c. Durante dies.

5 Significant Quotations

What is the importance of each of these quotations?

1. "After that, there would be perhaps several hours of delay before the sheriff gathered a sufficient posse and started on his trail."

2. "The windmill looked like a sacred emblem to Durante, and the twenty stodgy, tarpainted tanks blessed his eyes [...]."

3. "'What killed your father?' asked Durante."

4. "It was wine!"

5. "He seized his shirt at the throat and tore it away so that it hung in two rags from his hips."

2 COMPREHENSION ESSAY QUESTIONS

Use specific details and information from the story to answers these as completely as possible.

1. How does the story of Tony's father foreshadow this story? Use specific details and information from the story to support your answer.

2. What is the central irony in this story? Use specific details and information from the story to support your answer.

DISCUSSION QUESTIONS

Be prepared to discuss these in class.

1. How many ironies do you find in this story? Use specific details and information from the story to support your ideas.

2. Who do you think the protagonist and/or the antagonist is in this story? Use specific details and information from the story to support your thinking.

WRITING

Use each of these ideas for writing an essay.

1. This story is largely about friendship. Using specific examples, present instances that demonstrate a good friendship you have, or a bad one.

2. Water is essential to all of us for survival. Tony uses various machines—the tanks, the pumps, and so forth—to survive. Tell about one or two machines that you feel—seriously or humorously—you need to survive.

Further Writing

1. Alcohol drains the body fluids. Research the effects of alcohol on exercise and on bodily functions generally.

2. Compare and contrast the characters in this story to the characters in "The Cask of Amontillado" by Edgar Allan Poe (available in a library).

The Tell-Tale Heart

Edgar Allan Poe

PRE-READING VOCABULARY
CONTEXT

Use context clues to define these words before reading. Use a dictionary as needed.

1. The movie was so terrible that it was *dreadful. Dreadful* means

   _____.

2. The smell of dinner may *sharpen* one's appetite. *Sharpen* means

   _____.

3. After too much use, the knife became *dull. Dull* means

   _____.

4. A *vulture* circled overhead, waiting to eat the dead animal. *Vulture*

   means _____.

5. Not being able to separate reality from fantasy is just plain *mad. Mad*

   means _____.

6. To see down the dark hallway, Betty used a *lantern. Lantern* means

   _____.

7. The cat *cunningly* hid in the closet so that she could jump out and

   scare us. *Cunningly* means _____.

8. The sudden, loud noise *startled* Juan. *Startle* means

   _____.

9. Albert bought new wooden *shutters* to filter the light in each window.

   Shutter means _____.

10. Renée was in *awe* when she actually met the rock superstar. *Awe* means _____.

11. Shirley was *furious* when her dog tore up her favorite, brand new shoes. *Furious* means _____.

12. The smog *enveloped* the city making it very hard to see. *Envelop* means _____.

13. As he got tired of waiting, Jim's tapping fingers beat a continual *tattoo* on the countertop. *Tattoo* means _____.

14. When Kathy saw the mouse run across her foot, she let out a loud *shriek*. *Shriek* means _____.

15. John *muffled* the loud noise with earplugs. *Muffle* means

_____.

16. After the funeral, the *corpse* was buried in the old cemetery. *Corpse* means _____.

17. After running the mile, Aimée could feel her heart beat and sensed its every *pulsation*. *Pulsation* means _____.

18. The mechanic had to *dismember* the car to get to the fan belt. *Dismember* means _____.

19. After money suddenly was found to be continuously missing, we developed a *suspicion* that the new employee was stealing. *Suspicion* means _____.

20. Although Bruce was very upset after his accident, he *dissembled* well and had us all believing that he was not upset at all. *Dissemble* means _____.

PRE-READING VOCABULARY
STRUCTURAL ATTACK

Define these words by solving the parts. Use the Glossary or a dictionary as needed.

1. causeless
2. unperceived
3. stealthily
4. distinctness
5. motionless

6. uncontrollable
7. precaution
8. concealment
9. hastily

PRE-READING QUESTIONS

Try answering these questions as you read.

Who are the characters in the story?

How does the narrator want you to feel about him?

Sanity is defined as being able to recognize reality, while insanity is defined as not being able to recognize reality. What does this tell you about the narrator?

What hints does Poe give you for the startling ending?

The Tell-Tale Heart

EDGAR ALLAN POE

Edgar Allan Poe was born in 1809 and orphaned at a young age. He was adopted by John Allan, a rather militaristic businessman from Richmond, Virginia. Adoption by a person of means was not uncommon and would have been fortunate for the young Poe, except that his free spirit and his father's precision clashed. John Allan provided Poe with study at the University of Virginia—but Poe withdrew, due to drinking problems—and then at West Point—but Poe was dismissed, due to a disciplinary problem. Poe later married his very young cousin, Virginia Clemm, but the probable nonconsummation of this marriage and the early death of young Virginia contributed to Poe's idealization of both real and imagined women. His life, in fact, was one of continual disappointments. After Virginia's death, Poe sank into intermittent depressions, suffered bouts of insanity, and experienced hallucinations. Writing for many others, he wanted to publish his own magazine, but this dissolved in financial failure. He eventually died in Baltimore in 1849.

However, it is from these very problems that Poe's genius soars. He envelops the reader with his perceived worlds of the sane and insane, the rational and macabre, with equal ease. Credited with developing the modern mystery form, Poe uses every word and every action to draw the reader in, mixing reality with irreality, sane with insane. His other works include "The Pit and the Pendulum" and "The Fall of the House of Usher."

True! nervous—very, very dreadfully nervous I had been and am; but why *will* you say that I am mad? The disease had sharpened my senses—not destroyed—not dulled them. Above all was the sense of hearing acute. I heard all things in the heaven and in the earth. I heard many things in hell. How, then, am I mad? Hearken! and observe how healthily—how calmly I can tell you the whole story.

2   It is impossible to say how first the idea entered my brain; but once conceived, it haunted me day and night. Object there was none. Passion there was none. I loved the old man. He had never wronged me. He had never given me insult. For his gold I had no desire. I think it was his eye! yes, it was this! He had the eye of a vulture—a pale blue eye, with a film over it. Whenever it fell upon me, my blood ran cold; and so by degrees—very gradually—I made up my mind to take the life of the old man, and thus rid myself of the eye forever.

3   Now this is the point. You fancy me mad. Madmen know nothing. But you should have seen *me.* You should have seen how wisely I proceeded—with what caution—with what foresight—with what dissimulation I went to work! I was never kinder to the old man than during the whole week before I killed him. And every night, about midnight, I turned the latch of his door and opened it—ah, so gently! And then, when I had made an opening sufficient for my head, I put in a dark lantern, all closed, closed, so that no light shone out, and then I thrust in my head. Oh, you would have laughed to see how cunningly I thrust it in! I moved it slowly—very, very slowly, so that I might not disturb the old man's sleep. It took me an hour to place my whole head within the opening so far that I could see him as he lay upon his bed. Ha!—would a madman have been so wise as this? And then, when my head was well in the room, I undid the lantern cautiously—oh, so cautiously—cautiously (for the hinges creaked)—I undid it just so much that a single thin ray fell upon the vulture eye. And this I did for seven long nights—every night just at midnight—but I found the eye always closed; and so it was impossible to do the work; for it was not the old man who vexed me, but his Evil Eye. And every morning, when the day broke, I went boldly into the chamber, and spoke courageously to him, calling him by name in a hearty tone, and inquiring how he had passed the night. So you see he would have been a very profound old man, indeed, to suspect that every night, just at twelve, I looked in upon him while he slept.

4   Upon the eighth night I was more than usually cautious in opening the door. A watch's minute hand moves more quickly than did mine. Never, before that night, had I *felt* the extent of my own powers—of my sagacity. I could scarcely contain my feelings of triumph. To think that there I was, opening the door, little by little, and he not

even to dream of my secret deeds or thoughts. I fairly chuckled at the idea; and perhaps he heard me; for he moved on the bed suddenly, as if startled. Now you may think that I drew back—but no. His room was as black as pitch with the thick darkness (for the shutters were close fastened, through fear of robbers), and so I knew that he could not see the opening of the door, and I kept pushing it on steadily, steadily.

5   I had my head in, and was about to open the lantern, when my thumb slipped upon the tin fastening, and the old man sprang up in bed, crying out, "Who's there?" I kept quite still and said nothing. For a whole hour I did not move a muscle, and in the meantime I did not hear him lie down. He was still sitting up in the bed listening—just as I have done, night after night, hearkening to the death watches in the wall.

6   Presently I heard a slight groan, and I knew it was the groan of mortal terror. It was not a groan of pain or of grief—oh, no!—it was the low stifled sound that rises from the bottom of the soul when overcharged with awe. I knew the sound well. Many a night, just at midnight, when all the world slept, it has welled up from my own bosom, deepening, with its dreadful echo, the terrors that distracted me. I say I knew it well. I knew what the old man felt, and pitied him, although I chuckled at heart. I knew that he had been lying awake ever since the first slight noise, when he had turned in his bed. His fears had been ever since growing upon him. He had been trying to fancy them causeless, but could not. He had been saying to himself—"It is nothing but the wind in the chimney— it is only a mouse crossing the floor," or "It is merely a cricket which has made a single chirp." Yes, he had been trying to comfort himself with these suppositions: but he had found all in vain. *All in vain;* because Death, in approaching him, had stalked with his black shadow before him, and enveloped the victim. And it was the mournful influence of the unperceived shadow that caused him to feel—although he neither saw nor heard—to *feel* the presence of my head within the room.

7   When I had waited a long time, very patiently, without hearing him lie down, I resolved to open a little—a very, very little crevice in the lantern. So I opened it—you cannot imagine how stealthily, stealthily—until at length a single dim ray, like the thread of the spider, shot from out the crevice and fell upon the vulture eye.

8   It was open—wide, wide open—and I grew furious as I gazed upon it. I saw it with perfect distinctiveness—all a dull blue, with a hideous veil over it that chilled the very marrow in my bones; but I could see nothing else of the old man's face or person; for I had directed the ray as if by instinct, precisely upon the damned spot.

9   And have I not told you that what you mistake for madness is but overacuteness of the senses?—Now, I say, there came to my ears a low, dull, quick sound, such as a watch makes when enveloped in cotton.

I knew *that* sound well, too. It was the beating of the old man's heart. It increased my fury, as the beating of a drum stimulates the soldier into courage.

10   But even yet I refrained and kept still. I scarcely breathed. I held the lantern motionless. I tried how steadily I could maintain the ray upon the eye. Meantime the hellish tattoo of the heart increased. It grew quicker and quicker, and louder and louder every instant. The old man's terror *must* have been extreme! It grew louder, I say louder every moment!—do you mark me well? I have told you that I am nervous: so I am. And now at the dead hour of the night, amid the dreadful silence of that old house, so strange a noise as this excited me to uncontrollable terror. Yet, for some minutes longer I refrained and stood still. But the beating grew louder, louder. I thought the heart must burst. And now a new anxiety seized me—the sound would be heard by a neighbor! The old man's hour had come! With a loud yell, I threw open the lantern and leaped into the room. He shrieked once—once only. In an instant I dragged him to the floor, and pulled the heavy bed over him. I then smiled gaily, to find the deed so far done. But, for many minutes, the heart beat on with a muffled sound. This, however, did not vex me; it would not be heard through the wall. At length it ceased. The old man was dead. I removed the bed and examined the corpse. Yes, he was stone, stone dead. I placed my hand upon the heart and held it there many minutes. There was no pulsation. He was stone dead. His eye would trouble me no more.

11   If still you think me mad, you will think so no longer when I describe the wise precautions I took for the concealment of the body. The night waned, and I worked hastily, but in silence. First of all I dismembered the corpse. I cut off the head and the arms and the legs.

12   I then took up three planks from the flooring of the chamber, and deposited all between the scantlings. I then replaced the boards so cleverly, so cunningly, that no human eye—not even his—could have detected anything wrong. There was nothing to wash out—no stain of any kind—no blood spot whatever. I had been too wary for that. A tub had caught all—ha! ha!

13   When I had made an end of these labors, it was four o'clock—still dark as midnight. As the bell sounded the hour, there came a knocking at the street door. I went down to open it with a light heart—for what had I *now* to fear? There entered three men, who introduced themselves, with perfect suavity, as officers of the police. A shriek had been heard by a neighbor during the night; suspicion of foul play had been aroused; information had been lodged at the police office, and they (the officers) had been deputed to search the premises.

14   I smiled—for *what* had I to fear? I bade the gentlemen welcome. The shriek, I said, was my own in a dream. The old man, I mentioned, was absent in the country. I took my visitors all over the house. I bade them search—search *well*. I led them, at length, to *his* chamber. I showed them his treasures, secure, undisturbed. In the enthusiasm of my confidence, I brought chairs into the room, and desired them *here* to rest from their fatigues, while I myself, in the wild audacity of my perfect triumph, placed my own seat upon the very spot beneath which reposed the corpse of the victim.

15   The officers were satisfied. My *manner* had convinced them. I was singularly at ease. They sat, and while I answered cheerily, they chatted of familiar things. But, erelong, I felt myself getting pale and wished them gone. My head ached, and I fancied a ringing in my ears: but still they sat and still chatted. The ringing became more distinct—it continued and became more distinct; I talked more freely to get rid of the feeling; but it continued and gained definiteness—until, at length, I found that the noise was *not* within my ears.

16   No doubt I now grew *very* pale—but I talked more fluently, and with a heightened voice. Yet the sound increased—and what could I do? It was *a low, dull, quick sound—much such a sound as a watch makes when enveloped in cotton*. I gasped for breath—and yet the officers heard it not. I talked more quickly—more vehemently; but the noise steadily increased. I arose and argued about rifles, in a high key and with violent gesticulations; but the noise steadily increased. Why *would* they not be gone? I paced the floor to and fro with heavy strides, as if excited to fury by the observations of the men—but the noise steadily increased. Oh, God! what *could* I do? I foamed—I raved—I swore! I swung the chair upon which I had been sitting, and grated it upon the boards, but the noise arose over all and continually increased. It grew louder—louder—*louder!* And still the men chatted pleasantly, and smiled. Was it possible they heard not? Almighty God!—no, no! They heard!—they suspected!—they *knew!*—they were making a mockery of my horror!—this I thought, and this I think. But anything was better than this agony! Anything was more tolerable than derision! I could bear those hypocritical smiles no longer! I felt that I must scream or die! and now—again!—hark! louder! louder! louder! *louder!*

17   "Villains!" I shrieked, "dissemble no more! I admit the deed!—tear up the planks! here, here!—it is the beating of his hideous heart!"

The Tell-Tale Heart

JOURNAL

1. **MLA Works Cited**   *Using this model, record this story here.*

   Author's Last Name, First Name. "Title of the Story." *Title of the Book.*
   2nd ed. Ed. First Name Last Name. City: Publisher, year. Page number(s) of
   this story. Print.

2. **Main Character(s)**   *Describe each main character, and explain why you think each is a main character.*

3. **Supporting Characters**   *Describe each supporting character, and explain why you think each is a supporting character.*

4. **Setting and Props**   *Describe the setting(s) and all relevant prop(s).*

5. Sequence   *Outline the events of the story in order.*

6. Plot   *Tell the story in no more than two sentences.*

7. Conflicts   *Identify and explain all the conflicts involved here.*

8. Significant Quotations   *Explain the importance of each of these quotations. Record the page number in the parentheses.*

   a. "The disease had sharpened my senses—not destroyed—not dulled them" ( ).

   b. "He had the eye of a vulture—a pale blue eye, with a film over it"( ).

c. "Upon the eighth night I was more than usually cautious in opening the door" (   ).

d. "And have I not told you that what you mistake for madness is but overacuteness of the senses?—Now, I say, there came to my ears a low, dull, quick sound, such as a watch makes when enveloped in cotton" (   ).

e. "I gasped for breath—and yet the officers heard it not" (   ).

9. **Literary Elements**   *Look at this chapter's title and explain why you think this story is placed in this chapter. Explain in which other chapter(s) you might place this story, as relevant to the literary element(s) of that chapter.*

10. **Foreshadowing, Irony, and/or Symbolism**   *Explain examples of foreshadowing, irony, and/or symbolism in this story.*

Follow-up Questions
10 Short Questions

What is the <u>best</u> answer for each?

____ 1. The narrator thinks
    a. he is sane.
    b. he is insane.
    c. he is normal.

____ 2. The narrator wants you to think
    a. he is sane.
    b. he is insane.
    c. he is sane and more clever than most.

____ 3. At first, the narrator is
    a. kind to the old man.
    b. unkind to the old man.
    c. unfeeling toward the old man.

____ 4. The old man is
    a. unkind to the narrator.
    b. like a father figure to the narrator.
    c. the narrator's brother.

____ 5. The narrator probably shares
    a. no relationship with the old man.
    b. a formal working relationship with the old man.
    c. a family-like relationship with the old man.

____ 6. The narrator
    a. hates the old man.
    b. loves the old man.
    c. does not care about the old man.

____ 7. The narrator
    a. hates the old man's eye.
    b. loves the old man's eye.
    c. does not care about the old man's eye.

____ 8. The narrator
    a. has planned well.
    b. has not planned well.
    c. does not tell the reader about his plans.

____ 9. The only person(s) who can hear the heartbeat is (are)
    a. the police.
    b. the old man.
    c. the narrator.

____ 10. At first, the police
    a. do not suspect the narrator.
    b. do suspect the narrator.
    c. know the old man is dead.

5 Significant Quotations

What is the importance of each of these quotations?

1. "True! nervous—very, very dreadfully nervous I had been and am; but why *will* you say that I am mad?"

2. "I think it was his eye! yes, it was this!"

3. "You fancy me mad. Madmen know nothing. But you should have seen *me*."

4. "And this I did for seven long nights—every night just at midnight—but I found the eye always closed; and so it was important to do the work; [...]."

5. "'Villains!' I shrieked, 'dissemble no more! I admit the deed!—tear up the planks! here, here!—it is the beating of his hideous heart!'"

2 Comprehension Essay Questions

Use specific details and information from the story to answer these questions as completely as possible.

1. How does the title relate to the story? Explain the significance of the title using specific details and information from the story.

2. What are all the events that happens during the narrator's confession? Use specific details and information from the story for your explanation.

Discussion Questions

Be prepared to discuss these questions in class.

1. What characteristics of the homicidal mind do you think this story presents?

2. How does Poe's biography relate to this story? Use specific details from the biographical blurb and the story to support your ideas.

Writing

Use each of these ideas for writing an essay.

1. At one time or another, we have all been so scared that we could hear our own heartbeat. Tell the story of a time when you were so scared that you could hear your heartbeat.

2. The narrator is very sure that what he is doing is very clever. Describe a time when you or someone you know was sure of being right when, in fact, what you or she or he was doing was wrong.

Further Writing

1. Compare and contrast the narrator in this story with Montresor in Edgar Allan Poe's "The Cask of Amontillado" (available in a library).

2. Research today's use of the insanity plea in criminal actions. Poe's story offers an insightful anecdote for this study.

NOTES

CHAPTER 4

Irony

Irony is found in the difference between what *is* and what *should be.* Irony may be bitter—you work and work, and someone new, who has done nothing, arrives at your job and gets the promotion you deserve. Irony may be humorous—you wake up late and race around knowing you will be late for class, only to get to school and find out that your class has been canceled. Irony may even be providential—you sleep in and miss your bus, only to find out that the bus was in an accident and you are still safe at home. Think of ironies as unexpected twists in time, places, or events.

A story by O. Henry is a good example of irony. In the story, a gentleman treats a poor man to a Thanksgiving feast. In the end, both men end up in the hospital. The reader finds out that the poor man has had a big dinner before this second feast and is overfed. Meanwhile, the proud gentleman has spent his money on feeding this poor man who does not need more food, and the gentleman is underfed. The irony, of course, is that the man who does not need the food is overfed, while the man who does need the food goes without food.

Although all of the stories in this book present ironic twists, the stories in this chapter focus on irony. Ah Bah and Mrs. Mallard sustain true surprises in "Ah Bah's Money" and "The Story of an Hour," while Della and Jim turn gift giving upside down in "Gifts of the Magi." Remember Nathalie's assumed plan in "The Kiss" or Raju's good intentions in "Trail of the Green Blazer," Tom Sawyer's treasure trove in "Strong Temptations[...]" or Durante's fate in "Wine on the Desert" and you will be on your way to understanding irony.

Enjoy the twists here, and reflect on the ironies you have read in other stories—and on those you have experienced in your own life.

143

Ah Bah's Money

CATHERINE LIM

PRE-READING VOCABULARY
CONTEXT

Use context clues to define these words before reading. Use a dictionary as needed.

1. When she felt a sneeze coming on, Lisa looked for a *handkerchief* in her bag to cover up her sneeze. *Handkerchief* means

   _____.

2. Although it was a hot day, Ashley was *reluctant* to enter the pool after she tested the water and the water was too cold. *Reluctant* means

   _____.

3. When she wanted to take her toys with her, Caitlin took out a cloth and put the toys in it, making a *bundle* she could carry. *Bundle* means _____.

4. When Bonnie graduated from college, she took a job so that she could *earn* enough money to support herself. *Earn* means _____.

5. John was very confident in the electrician he hired and felt *secure* that the electrician did a good job. *Secure* means _____.

6. When she bought new dishes, Jamie also bought a large *cupboard* for the dining room that would show off her new dishes. *Cupboard* means

   _____.

7. When Teddy bought his Mercedes, he treated it like a *treasure,* polishing it and keeping it as good as new. *Treasure* means

   _____.

8. When the fraternity house planned a party, the members bought potato chips to eat and a lot of *beer* to drink. *Beer* means

_____.

9. Carrie was *terrified* of spiders and would yell for her mother to drop everything and come kill the spider. *Terrified* means

_____.

10. Rajan became very *dispirited* when he worked hard to solve a problem and then his boss stole the credit from Rajan. *Dispirited* means

_____.

11. Chinese people celebrate the New Year by giving children *ang pows*, which are little red bags filled with money. *Ang pow* means

_____.

12. Jess was delighted when she won the lottery and had many ideas on how to spend her newfound *wealth*. *Wealth* means

_____.

13. When Reid's team won the game, his joy was *conspicuous* in the large smile that lit up his entire face. *Conspicuous* means

_____.

14. When Li Qin wadded up all her paper money in a big roll, it made a *bulge* in her pocket that everyone could see. *Bulge* means _____.

15. When Tricia took the little two-year-old to the toy store, the child *bawled* and cried and carried on when he didn't get the toy he wanted. *Bawl* means _____.

16. Not being able to solve a problem can cause a great deal of frustration and *vexation*. *Vexation* means _____.

17. When Xi Ling ruined her shoes by walking in the rain, her mother *scolded* her for ruining her shoes. *Scold* means _____.

18. With no planning and without even thinking first, Margaret bought a lottery ticket on *impulse* and won the big prize. *Impulse* means

_____.

19. Bob showed great *ingenuity* when he cleverly solved the problem that others could not solve. *Ingenuity* means _____.

20. When Ben lost his wallet, it was a great *loss*, not only because of the money he lost but also because of the time he lost trying to find it. *Loss* means _____.

Pre-reading Vocabulary
Structural Attack

Define these words by solving the parts. Use the Glossary or a dictionary as needed.

1. greenish	12. feverishly
2. thereafter	13. bitterly
3. uneasy	14. bedroom
4. broken-down	15. miserably
5. endlessly	16. successfully
6. bad-tempered	17. triumphantly
7. indifferent	18. amazement
8. forefinger	19. firewood
9. expertly	20. restless
10. immediately	21. aching
11. frantically	22. quietened

Pre-reading Questions

Try answering these questions as you read.

How does Ah Bah hide his money?

From whom is he hiding his money?

What is ironic here?

Ah Bah's Money

Catherine Lim

Catherine Lim was born in Malaya but continued her schooling in Singapore. She first taught and then became an administrator, developing curriculum materials for elementary school children. She later became a writer, focusing on and even satirizing life in Singapore. More of her stories can be found in *Little Ironies: Stories of Singapore.*

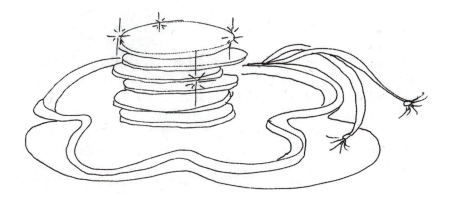

Ah Bah's money, in 2 one-dollar notes and an assortment of coins, lay in a pile on the old handkerchief, but Ah Bah was reluctant to pull up the corners into a bundle to put inside the cigarette tin. Ah Bah was reluctant because the sight of his money gave him so much pleasure. He had already done the following things with his money: spread out the notes and arranged the coins in a row beside them, stacked up the coins according to their denominations, stacked up the coins to make each stack come to a dollar. But still he wanted to go on touching his money. He could tell exactly which coin came from whom or where. The twenty-cent coin with the greenish stain on the edge was given to him by Ah Lam Soh, who was opening her purse when the coin dropped out and he picked it up for her.

2 "You may keep it," she said, and thereafter Ah Bah watched closely every time Ah Lam Soh opened her purse or put her hand into her blouse pocket. The ten-cent coin, which had a better shine than all the rest, he had actually found near a rubbish dump, almost hidden from sight by an old slipper. And the largest coin of all, the fifty-cent coin, he had earned. He was still rather puzzled about why Kim Heok Soh had given him so much money; he had been required merely to stand in the front portion of the house and to say to any visitor, "Kim

Heok Soh has gone to the dry goods shop and will not be back till an hour later. She has asked me to take care of her house for her." But all the time Kim Heok Soh was in the house; he knew because he could hear her in the room and there was somebody with her.

3   He counted his money—five dollars and eighty-five cents, and his heart glowed. Very carefully, he pulled up the corners of the handkerchief at last into a tight bundle which he then put inside the cigarette tin. Then he put the cover on firmly, and his money, now safe and secure, was ready to go back into its hiding place in a corner of the cupboard behind the stacks of old clothes, newspapers and calendars.

4   And now Ah Bah became uneasy, and he watched to see if his father's eyes would rest on the old broken-down cupboard that held his treasure, for once his father had found his money—two dollars in twenty- and ten-cent coins—tied up in a piece of rag and hidden under his pillow, and had taken it away for another bottle of beer. His father drank beer almost every night. Sometimes he was in a good mood after his beer and he would talk endlessly about this or that, smiling to himself. But generally he became sullen and bad-tempered, and he would begin shouting at anyone who came near. Once he threw an empty beer bottle at Ah Bah's mother; it missed her head and went crashing against the wall. Ah Bah was terrified of his father, but his mother appeared indifferent. "The lunatic," she would say, but never in his hearing. Whenever he was not at home, she would slip out and play cards in Ah Lam Soh's house. One evening she returned, flushed with excitement and gave him fifty cents; she said it had been her lucky day. At other times she came back with a dispirited look, and Ah Bah knew she had lost all her money in Ah Lam Soh's house.

5   The New Year was coming and Ah Bah looked forward to it with an intensity that he could barely conceal. New Year meant *ang pows*; Ah Bah's thin little fingers closed round the red packets of money given him by the New Year visitors with such energy that his mother would scold him and shake her head in doleful apology, as she remarked loudly to the visitors, "My Ah Bah, he feels no shame whatever!"

6   His forefinger and thumb feeling expertly through the red paper, Ah Bah could tell immediately how much was in the red packet; his heart would sink a little if the fingers felt the hard edges of coins, for that would be forty cents or eighty cents at most. But if nothing was felt, then joy of joys! Here was at least a dollar inside.

7   This year Ah Bah had *eight* dollar notes. He could hardly believe it when he took stock of his wealth on the last day of the festive season. Eight new notes, crisp, still smelling new, and showing no creases except where they had been folded to go into the red packets. Eight

dollars! And a small pile of coins besides. Ah Bah experienced a thrill such as he had never felt before.

8   And then it was all anxiety and fear, for he realized that his father knew about his *ang pow* money; indeed his father had referred to it once or twice, and would, Ah Bah was certain, be searching the bedding, cupboard and other places in the house for it.

9   Ah Bah's heart beat with the violence of angry defiance at the thought. The total amount in his cigarette tin was now seventeen dollars and twenty-five cents, and Ah Bah was determined to protect his money at all costs. Nobody was going to take his money from him. Frantically, Ah Bah went to the cupboard, took out the bundle of money from the cigarette tin and stuffed it into his trouser pocket. It made a conspicuous bulge. Ah Bah didn't know what to do, and his little mind worked feverishly to find a way out of this very direful situation.

10   He was wandering about in the village the next day as usual, and when he returned home, he was crying bitterly. His pocket was empty. When his mother came to him and asked him what the matter was, he bawled. He told her, between sobs, that a rough-looking Indian had pushed him to the ground and taken away his money. His father who was in the bedroom rushed out, and made Ah Bah tell again what had happened. When Ah Bah had finished, sniffling miserably, his father hit him on the head, snarling, "You idiot! Why were you so anxious to show off your *ang pow* money? Now you've lost it all!" And when he was told that the sum was seventeen dollars and twenty-five cents, his vexation was extreme, so that he would not be contented till he had hit the boy again.

11   Ah Bah's mother cleaned the bruise on the side of his face where he had been pushed to the ground, and led him away from his father.

12   "You are a silly boy," she scolded. "Why did you carry so much money around with you? Someone was sure to rob you!" And feeling sorry for him, she felt about in her blouse pocket and found she could spare fifty cents, so she gave it to him, saying, "Next time, don't be so silly, son."

13   He took the coin from her, and he was deeply moved. And then, upon impulse, he took her by the hand, and led her outside their house to the old hen-house, near the well, under the trees, and he whispered to her, his heart almost bursting with the excitement of a portentous secret successfully kept, "It's there! In the cigarette tin, behind that piece of wood!" To prove it, he squeezed into the hen house and soon emerged, reeking of hen house odors, triumphantly clutching the tin. He took off the lid and showed her the money inside.

14   She was all amazement. Then she began to laugh and to shake her head over the ingenuity of it all, while he stood looking up at her, his eyes bright and bold with victory.

15   "You're a clever boy," she said, "but take care that you don't go near the hen house often. Your father's pocket is empty again, and he's looking around to see whose money he can get hold of, that devil."

16   Ah Bah earned twenty cents helping Ah Lau Sim to scrape coconut, and his mother allowed him to have the ten cents which he found on a shelf, under a comb. Clutching his money, he stole out of the house; he was just in time to back out of the hen house, straighten himself and pretend to be looking for dried twigs for firewood, for his father stood at the doorway, looking at him. His father was in a restless mood again, pacing the floor with a dark look on his face, and this was the sign that he wanted his beer very badly but had no money to pay for it. Ah Bah bent low, assiduously looking for firewood, and then through the corner of his eye, he saw his father go back into the house.

17   That night Ah Bah dreamt that his father had found out the hiding place in the hen house, and early next morning, his heart beating wildly, he stole out and went straight to the hen house. He felt about in the darkness for his cigarette tin; his hand touched the damp of the hen droppings and caught on a nail, and still he searched—but the cigarette tin was not there.

18   He ran sniffling to his mother, and she began to scold him, "I told you not to go there too often, but you wouldn't listen to me. Didn't you know your father has been asking for money? The devil's found you out again!"

19   The boy continued to sniff, his little heart aching with the terrible pain of the loss.

20   "Never mind," his mother said, "you be a good boy and don't say anything about it; otherwise your father's sure to rage like a mad man." She led him inside the house and gave him a slice of bread with some sugar.

21   She was glad when he quietened down at last, for she didn't want to keep Ah Lam Soh and the others waiting. The seventeen dollars and twenty-five cents (she had hurriedly hidden the handkerchief and the cigarette tin) was secure in her blouse pocket, and she slipped away with eager steps for, as the fortune teller had told her, this was the beginning of a period of good luck for her.

Ah Bah's Money

JOURNAL

1. **MLA Works Cited**   *Using this model, record this story here.*

   Author's Last Name, First Name. "Title of the Story." *Title of the Book.*

   2nd ed. Ed. First Name Last Name. City: Publisher, year. Page number(s)

   of this story. Print.

2. **Main Character(s)**   *Describe each main character, and explain why you think each is a main character.*

3. **Supporting Characters**   *Describe each supporting character, and explain why you think each is a supporting character.*

4. **Setting and Props**   *Describe the setting(s) and all relevant prop(s).*

5. **Sequence**   *Outline the events of the story in order.*

6. **Plot**   *Tell the story in no more than two sentences.*

7. **Conflicts**   *Identify and explain all the conflicts involved here.*

8. **Significant Quotations**   *Explain the importance of each quotation completely. Record the page number in the parentheses.*

   a. "Ah Bah was reluctant because the sight of his money gave him so much pleasure" (   ).

   b. "And now Ah Bah became uneasy, and he watched to see if his father's eyes would rest on the old broken-down cupboard that held his treasure, for once his father had found his money—[…]" (   ).

c. "Frantically, Ah Bah went to the cupboard, took out the bundle of money from cigarette tin and stuffed it into his trouser pocket" (   ).

d. "To prove it, he squeezed into the hen house and soon emerged, reeking of hen house odors, triumphantly clutching the tin" (   ).

e. "She was glad when he quietened down at last, for she didn't want to keep Ah Lam Soh and the others waiting" (   ).

9. **Literary Elements**   *Look at this chapter's title and explain why you think this story is placed in this chapter. Explain in which other chapter(s) you might place this story, as relevant to the literary element(s) of the chapter(s).*

10. **Foreshadowing, Irony, and/or Symbols**   *Explain examples of foreshadowing, irony, and/or symbols in this story.*

Follow-up Questions

10 SHORT QUESTIONS

What is the <u>best</u> answer for each?

____ 1. Ah Bah's money
   a. is very important to him.
   b. does not concern him.
   c. is easy for him to hide.

____ 2. Ah Bah's money
   a. is all earned by him.
   b. comes from gifts and earnings.
   c. all comes from gifts.

____ 3. Ah Bah
   a. always keeps his money behind the cupboard.
   b. works hard at hiding his money.
   c. always keeps his money in the same place.

____ 4. Ah Bah
   a. is never sure how much money he has.
   b. sometimes is not sure how much money he has.
   c. almost always knows exactly how much money he has.

____ 5. Ah Bah's father
   a. gives Ah Bah money.
   b. wants Ah Bah's money.
   c. does not know about Ah Bah's money.

____ 6. Ah Bah's father
   a. is a drinker.
   b. is kind to Ah Bah.
   c. is generous to Ah Bah.

____ 7. Ah Bah
   a. always keeps his money behind the cupboard.
   b. is sure his father does not know about his money.
   c. tries to hide his money in the hen house.

____ 8. Ah Bah tells
   a. no one about the hen house.
   b. his mother about the hen house.
   c. his father about the hen house.

____ 9. Ah Bah's mother
   a. warns Ah Bah against his father.
   b. gives Ah Bah a safe hiding place.
   c. deserves Ah Bah's trust.

____ 10. In the end, Ah Bah's money
   a. is safe.
   b. is taken by his father.
   c. is taken by his mother.

5 SIGNIFICANT QUOTATIONS

What is the importance of each of these quotations?

1. "He could tell exactly which coin came from whom or where."

2. "Then he put the cover on firmly, and his money, now safe and secure, was ready to go back into its hiding place in a corner of the cupboard [...]."

3. "His father drank beer almost every night."

4. "And then, upon impulse, he took her by the hand, and led her outside their house to the old hen house […]."

5. "He ran sniffling to his mother, and she began to scold him, 'I told you not to go there too often […]. Didn't you know your father has been asking for money?'"

2 Comprehension Essay Questions

Use specific details and information from the story to answer these questions as completely as possible.

1. What characteristics mark Ah Bah? His father? His mother? Use specific details and information from the story to support your descriptions.

2. What is the irony in this story? Use specific details and information from the story to support your answer.

Discussion Questions

Be prepared to discuss these questions in class.

1. How would you describe Ah Bah? His father? His mother?

2. What is ironic here?

Writing

Use each of these ideas for writing an essay.

1. Certainly, Ah Bah has a problem with people he trusts. Tell of a time that you or someone you know has been cheated by someone you or your friend trusted.

2. Ah Bah treasures his money, yet we all have things we especially treasure. Focus on some special thing that you or someone you know truly treasures. Tell the story of what makes this object so special.

Further Writing

1. Although this story is told with a very light touch, it brings up the very serious topic of addiction. Research alcoholism, drug abuse, and/or gambling addiction and apply your research to this story.

2. This story also demonstrates some of the dysfunctional dynamics found in families impacted by addiction. Research the psychosocial dynamics of addictive families and relate your research to this story.

The Story of an Hour
KATE CHOPIN

PRE-READING VOCABULARY
CONTEXT

Use context clues to define these words before reading. Use a dictionary as needed.

1. Susan was *afflicted* with a need to shop at the mall every weekend. *Afflicted* means _____.

2. The horrible earthquake caused major *disasters*, such as gas explosions and buildings collapsing, that resulted in injuries and deaths. *Disaster* means _____.

3. Before there were telephones, Jacob had to go to an office and send a *telegram* with news. *Telegram* means _____.

4. Evelyn tried to *hasten* Kristin so that she could get to school on time. *Hasten* means _____.

5. After the children lost their beloved dog, they suffered much *grief* and cried for days. *Grief* means _____.

6. The little leaves were all *aquiver* as the breeze blew through the tree. *Aquiver* means _____.

7. Some people are never allowed to laugh; they suffer severe *repression* when they see something funny. *Repression* means

    _____.

8. When Dottie did not understand the directions, her face became *vacant* with no expression. *Vacant* means

    _____.

9. The puppy had a *keen* sense of smell and could scent a hamburger a mile away. *Keen* means _____.

10. Blood *pulses* through our veins with a steady beat. *Pulse* means

_____.

11. The king held the most *exalted* position in the realm. *Exalted* means _____.

12. In the Macy's *procession,* colorful floats followed one after another. *Procession* means _____.

13. The host opened the door and warmly *welcomed* each guest as he or she arrived. *Welcome* means _____.

14. Without thinking about it, Kirk followed his *impulse* and suddenly bet all his chips on red. *Impulse* means _____.

15. When Bill thinks he is right, he answers with enough confidence and *self-assertion* to convince others he is correct. *Self-assertion* means _____.

16. Nancy *implored* the builder to start her deck as soon as possible before the rains came. *Implore* means _____.

17. A substance that can change base metals into gold, that can make one live forever, or that allows one to taste the very best of life is called an *elixir. Elixir* means _____.

18. Daren *shuddered* at the thought of having to take another algebra test. *Shudder* means _____.

19. The Cougars yelled, screamed, and jumped in *triumph* when they won the game. *Triumph* means _____.

20. Margaret was absolutely *amazed* when she won the ten-million-dollar lottery. *Amazed* means _____.

Pre-reading Vocabulary
Structural Attack

Define these words by solving the parts. Use the Glossary or a dictionary as needed.

1. inability
2. bespoke
3. fearfully
4. powerless
5. fellow-creatures

6. illumination
7. keyhole
8. feverish
9. latchkey
10. travel-stained

Pre-reading Questions

Try answering these questions as you read.

What happens to Mr. Mallard?

How does Mrs. Mallard feel?

What happens to Mrs. Mallard?

What is ironic in the story?

The Story of an Hour

KATE CHOPIN

Kate O'Flaherty Chopin was born in St. Louis, Missouri, in 1851 to an affluent family. Although her father died when she was young, her widowed mother gave young Kate a taste of female independence. In 1870 Kate married Oscar Chopin and moved to New Orleans and then to Natchitoches Parish. Here she met the Creoles, Acadians, and African Americans she would later write about. However, Oscar died in 1882, and by 1884 she sold the plantation, gathered her five children, and returned home to St. Louis, where she began to write for popular women's magazines. Influenced noticeably by Guy de Maupassant's sense of irony and Henrik Ibsen's social comment, Chopin wrote stories, often touched with rich symbols and images of nature, that question societal assumptions and dictates. *The Awakening* remains her masterwork, although short stories offer Chopin at her most terse. Chopin died in 1904.

Knowing that Mrs. Mallard was afflicted with a heart trouble, great care was taken to break to her as gently as possible the news of her husband's death.

2   It was her sister Josephine who told her, in broken sentences; veiled hints that revealed in half concealing. Her husband's friend Richards was there, too, near her. It was he who had been in the newspaper office when intelligence of the railroad disaster was received, with Brently Mallard's name leading the list of "killed." He had only taken the time to assure himself of its truth by a second telegram, and had hastened to forestall any less careful, less tender friend in bearing the sad message.

3   She did not hear the story as many women have heard the same, with a paralyzed inability to accept its significance. She wept at once, with sudden, wild abandonment, in her sister's arms. When the storm of grief had spent itself she went away to her room alone. She would have no one follow her.

4   There stood, facing the open window, a comfortable, roomy armchair. Into this she sank, pressed down by a physical exhaustion that haunted her body and seemed to reach into her soul.

5   She could see in the open square before her house the tops of trees that were all aquiver with the new spring life. The delicious breath of rain was in the air. In the street below a peddler was crying his wares. The notes of a distant song which some one was singing reached her faintly, and countless sparrows were twittering in the eaves.

6   There were patches of blue sky showing here and there through the clouds that had met and piled one above the other in the west facing her window.

7   She sat with her head thrown back upon the cushion of the chair, quite motionless, except when a sob came up into her throat and shook her, as a child who has cried itself to sleep continues to sob in its dreams.

8   She was young, with a fair, calm face, whose lines bespoke repression and even a certain strength. But now there was a dull stare in her eyes, whose gaze was fixed away off yonder on one of those patches of blue sky. It was not a glance of reflection, but rather indicated a suspension of intelligent thought.

9   There was something coming to her and she was waiting for it, fearfully. What was it? She did not know; it was too subtle and elusive to name. But she felt it, creeping out of the sky, reaching toward her through the sounds, the scents, the color that filled the air.

10   Now her bosom rose and fell tumultuously. She was beginning to recognize this thing that was approaching to possess her, and she was striving to beat it back with her will—as powerless as her two white slender hands would have been.

11   When she abandoned herself a little whispered word escaped her slightly parted lips. She said it over and over under her breath: "free, free, free!" The vacant stare and the look of terror that had followed it went from her eyes. They stayed keen and bright. Her pulses beat fast, and the coursing blood warmed and relaxed every inch of her body.

12   She did not stop to ask if it were or were not a monstrous joy that held her. A clear and exalted perception enabled her to dismiss the suggestion as trivial.

13   She knew that she would weep again when she saw the kind, tender hands folded in death; the face that had never looked save

with love upon her, fixed and gray and dead. But she saw beyond that bitter moment a long procession of years to come that would belong to her absolutely. And she opened and spread her arms out to them in welcome.

14   There would be no one to live for her during those coming years; she would live for herself. There would be no powerful will bending hers in that blind persistence with which men and women believe they have a right to impose a private will upon a fellow-creature. A kind intention or a cruel intention made the act seem no less a crime as she looked upon it in that brief moment of illumination.

15   And yet she had loved him—sometimes. Often she had not. What did it matter! What could love, the unsolved mystery, count for in the face of this possession of self-assertion which she suddenly recognized as the strongest impulse of her being!

16   "Free! Body and soul free!" she kept whispering.

17   Josephine was kneeling before the closed door with her lips to the keyhole, imploring for admission. "Louise, open the door! I beg; open the door—you will make yourself ill. What are you doing, Louise? For heaven's sake open the door."

18   "Go away. I am not making myself ill." No; she was drinking in a very elixir of life through that open window.

19   Her fancy was running riot along those days ahead of her. Spring days, and summer days, and all sorts of days that would be her own. She breathed a quick prayer that life might be long. It was only yesterday she had thought with a shudder that life might be long.

20   She arose at length and opened the door to her sister's importunities. There was a feverish triumph in her eyes, and she carried herself unwittingly like a goddess of Victory. She clasped her sister's waist, and together they descended the stairs. Richards stood waiting for them at the bottom.

21   Someone was opening the front door with a latchkey. It was Brently Mallard who entered, a little travel-stained, composedly carrying his grip-sack and umbrella. He had been far from the scene of the accident, and did not even know there had been one. He stood amazed at Josephine's piercing cry; at Richards' quick motion to screen him from the view of his wife.

22   But Richards was too late.

23   When the doctors came they said she had died of heart disease—of joy that kills.

The Story of an Hour
Journal

1. **MLA Works Cited**   *Using this model, record this story here.*

   Author's Last Name, First Name. "Title of the Story." *Title of the Book*

      2nd ed. Ed. First Name Last Name. City: Publisher, year. Page number(s)

      of this story. Print.

2. **Main Character(s)**   *Describe each main character, and explain why you think each is a main character.*

3. **Supporting Characters**   *Describe each supporting character, and explain why you think each is a supporting character.*

4. **Setting and Props**   *Describe the setting(s) and all relevant prop(s).*

5. **Sequence**   *Outline the events of the story in order.*

6. **Plot**   *Tell the story in no more than two sentences.*

7. **Conflicts**   *Identify and explain all the conflicts involved here.*

8. **Significant Quotations**   *Explain the importance of each of these quotations. Record the page number in the parentheses.*

   a. "Knowing that Mrs. Mallard was afflicted with a heart trouble, great care was taken to break to her as gently as possible the news of her husband's death" (   ).

   b. "When the storm of grief had spent itself she went away to her room alone" (   ).

    c. "She could see in the open square before her house the tops of trees that were all aquiver with the new spring life" (   ).

    d. "When she abandoned herself a little whispered word escaped her slightly parted lips. She said it over and over under her breath: 'free, free, free!'" (   ).

    e. "Someone was opening the door with a latchkey" (   ).

9. **Literary Elements**   *Look at this chapter's title and explain why you think this story is placed in this chapter. Explain in which other chapter(s) you might place this story, as relevant to the literary element(s) of that chapter.*

10. **Foreshadowing, Irony, and/or Symbolism**   *Explain examples of foreshadowing, irony, and/or symbolism in this story.*

Follow-up Questions

10 SHORT QUESTIONS

What is the __best__ answer for each?

____ 1. The person to first hear the news of the accident is
   a. Mrs. Mallard.
   b. Josephine.
   c. Richards.

____ 2. S/he hears the news
   a. at the railroad station.
   b. at the newspaper office.
   c. at home.

____ 3. Josephine and Richards are at the Mallard house
   a. to awaken Mrs. Mallard.
   b. to have lunch with Mrs. Mallard.
   c. to tell Mrs. Mallard about the accident.

____ 4. Mrs. Mallard is immediately
   a. overwhelmed.
   b. overjoyed.
   c. unimpressed.

____ 5. Mrs. Mallard
   a. goes to her room.
   b. stays with her sister.
   c. makes lunch.

____ 6. Mrs. Mallard slowly
   a. cries.
   b. faints.
   c. whispers "free."

____ 7. Mrs. Mallard
   a. always loved Brently Mallard.
   b. did not always love Brently Mallard.
   c. was looking forward to Brently Mallard's return.

____ 8. Brently Mallard
   a. was at home all the time.
   b. was in the accident.
   c. was not in the accident.

____ 9. Brently Mallard
   a. does come home.
   b. does not come home.
   c. is dead.

____ 10. Mrs. Mallard is
   a. delighted by his return.
   b. unmoved by his return.
   c. destroyed by his return.

5 SIGNIFICANT QUOTATIONS

What is the importance of each of these quotations?

1. "Knowing that Mrs. Mallard was afflicted with a heart condition, great care was taken to break to her as gently as possible the news of her husband's death."

2. "She wept at once, with sudden, wild abandonment, in her sister's arms."

3. "There was something coming to her and she was waiting for it, fearfully."

4. "She breathed a quick prayer that life might be long. It was only yesterday she had thought with a shudder that life might be long."

5. "When the doctors came they said she had died of heart disease—of joy that kills."

2 COMPREHENSION ESSAY QUESTIONS

Use specific details and information from the story to answer these questions as completely as possible.

1. How does the title relate to the story? Explain the significance of the title using specific details and information from the story.

2. What does the phrase "of joy that kills" mean? Use specific details and information from the story in your explanation.

DISCUSSION QUESTIONS

Be prepared to discuss these questions in class.

1. What does this story tell you about assumptions concerning husbands and wives? Use specific details from the story to support your ideas.

2. For which character do you feel more sympathy? Why?

WRITING

Use each of these ideas for writing an essay.

1. We have all tried to cover up our feelings at one time or another. Tell the story of a time you or someone you know used pleasure or sorrow to cover up real feelings about a situation or event. Pay special attention in your narrative to the reactions of others.

2. We have all made mistakes about how we think others feel. Sometimes these misunderstandings are quite humorous. Describe a time when you or someone you know assumed the wrong thing about someone else's feelings.

Further Writing

1. Discuss the similarities between Mrs. Mallard in this story and Calixta in Kate Chopin's "The Storm" (available in a library).

2. Discuss the similarities between Mrs. Mallard in this story and Nathalie in Kate Chopin's "The Kiss" (page 50).

3. Discuss the similarities between Mrs. Mallard in this story and Mrs. Alving in Henrik Ibsen's *Ghosts* (available in a library).

Gifts of the Magi

O. Henry

PRE-READING VOCABULARY
CONTEXT

Use context clues to define these words before reading. Use a dictionary as needed.

1. Sam was always cheap and never paid for anything he didn't have to, as a result of his *parsimony*. *Parsimony* means

    _____.

2. Rajan would never live in a *shabby* little shack and always demands the best in life. *Shabby* means _____.

3. Patricia owns and maintains her home and is truly the *mistress* of her house. *Mistress* means _____.

4. Laura likes only the very fine and beautiful—the most *sterling*—things in life. *Sterling* means _____.

5. Baby Alex has many *possessions*, including toys, books, trains, beautiful clothes, and a sun-filled room. *Possession* means

    _____.

6. At Niagara Falls, the water comes *cascading* down the falls at the rate of thousands of gallons each minute. *Cascading* means

    _____.

7. Cy went *ransacking* through his closet trying to find his favorite fraternity T-shirt that was lost. *Ransack* means

    _____.

8. Ted attached a *fob chain* to his pocket watch so that it would hang out of his vest pocket for all to see. *Fob chain* means

    _____.

9. The town suffered the *ravages* of war with burned-down buildings and blown-apart streets. *Ravage* means _____.

10. In past times, being a dancer in a line as a *chorus girl* was looked on as a lowly job only for loose women. *Chorus girl* means

_____.

11. Sundeep was *terrified* of snakes and would faint at the sight of one. *Terrified* means _____.

12. Bernie has the most *peculiar* laugh and no one else in the world can laugh the way he does. *Peculiar* means _____.

13. The men who came to visit baby Jesus and who brought precious gifts were considered to be wise and were called the *magi*. *Magi* means

_____.

14. George was *ecstatic* when his name was called as the winner of the lottery. *Ecstatic* means _____.

15. Stu became *hysterical* and had to be calmed down when he learned his cat had suddenly died. *Hysterical* means _____.

16. After Lori took the medicine, her headache *vanished,* and she felt fine. *Vanish* means _____.

17. Trish loves hot fudge sundaes and absolutely *craves* one when she hasn't had one in a long time. *Crave* means _____.

18. Nicole had wonderfully thick hair, and she took very special care of her beautiful *tresses*. *Tress* means _____.

19. The newborn Jesus may be referred to as the *Babe in the manger*. *Babe in the manger* means _____.

20. Simon *sacrificed* his free time to help teach the students how to write poetry. *Sacrifice* means _____.

Pre-reading Vocabulary
Structural Attack

Define these words by solving the parts. Use the Glossary or a dictionary as needed.

1. bulldozing
2. predominating
3. subsiding
4. furnished
5. blurred
6. airshaft
7. rippling
8. nervously
9. ornamentation
10. close-lying
11. critically
12. overcoat
13. immovable
14. fixedly
15. laboriously
16. mathematician
17. illumination
18. necessitating
19. lamely

Pre-reading Questions

Try answering these questions as you read.

What does Della sell?

What does Della buy?

What does Jim sell?

What does Jim buy?

What is ironic in the story?

Gifts of the Magi

O. Henry

William Sydney Porter was born in 1862 to an educated and a comfortable family living in Greensboro, North Carolina, and he grew up in the Reconstruction South. As a result of his mother's early death and his father's alcoholism, he was raised by his aunt, who gave him a love for narration. Like his father, he became a pharmacist's apprentice, and although he did not like the work, his uncle's drugstore provided him with a good vantage point from which to observe the townspeople. In 1882 he married Athol Estes Roach, settled into work at the National Bank of Texas, and bought a printing press to publish his stories in the short-lived *Rolling Stone*. He was charged and cleared of embezzlement—a charge he consistently denied. Later, faced with retrial, he fled to New Orleans and then to Honduras, all the while observing others. Returning to Texas because of his wife's failing health and subsequent death, he was retried and sent to the Ohio state penitentiary, where he served three years of a five-year sentence. Although it was a dark period in his life, he was again observing and, perhaps, gained his compassion for the underdog, as well as the pen name "O. Henry." In 1902 he moved to New York City to produce weekly stories for the *New York Sunday World,* and at the turn of the century and amid the streets of New York, which were largely filled with immigrants, he found endless stock for his stories. O. Henry died in 1910.

His stories are marked by concise characterizations, concern for working women and the poor, adroit wit, and succinct irony. His many stories and selected sketches are largely based on kernels from his real-life observations and are available in many collections.

One dollar and eighty-seven cents. That was all. And 60 cents of it was in pennies. Pennies saved one and two at a time by bulldozing the grocer and the vegetable man and the butcher until one's cheeks burned with the silent imputation of parsimony that such close dealing implied. Three times Della counted it. One dollar and eighty-seven cents. And the next day would be Christmas.

2   There was clearly nothing to do but flop down on the shabby little couch and howl. So Della did it. Which instigates the moral reflection that life is made up of sobs, sniffles and smiles, with sniffles predominating.

3   While the mistress of the home is gradually subsiding from the first stage to the second, take a look at the home. A furnished flat at $8 per week. It did not exactly beggar description, but it certainly had that word on the lookout for the mendicancy squad.

4   In the vestibule below belonged to this flat a letter-box into which no letter would go, and an electric button from which no mortal finger could coax a ring. Also appertaining thereunto was a card bearing the name "Mr. James Dillingham Young."

5   The "Dillingham" had been flung to the breeze during a former period of prosperity when its possessor was being paid $30 per week. Now, when the income was shrunk to $20, the letters of "Dillingham" looked blurred, as though they were thinking seriously of contracting to a modest and unassuming D. But whenever Mr. James Dillingham Young came home and reached his flat above he was called "Jim" and greatly hugged by Mrs. James Dillingham Young, already introduced to you as Della. Which is all very good.

6   Della finished her cry and attended to her cheeks with the powder rag. She stood by the window and looked out dully at a gray cat walking a gray fence in a gray backyard. Tomorrow would be Christmas Day, and she had only $1.87 with which to buy Jim a present. She had been saving every penny she could for months, with this result. Twenty dollars a week doesn't go far. Expenses had been greater than she had calculated. They always are. Only $1.87 to buy a present for Jim. Her Jim. Many a happy hour she had spent planning for something nice for him. Something fine and rare and sterling—something just a little bit near to being worthy of the honor of being owned by Jim.

7   There was a pier-glass between the windows of the room. Perhaps you have seen a pier-glass in an $8 flat. A very thin and very agile person may, by observing his reflection in a rapid sequence of longitudinal strips, obtain a fairly accurate conception of his looks. Della, being slender, had mastered the art.

8   Suddenly she whirled from the window and stood before the glass. Her eyes were shining brilliantly, but her face had lost its color within twenty seconds. Rapidly she pulled down her hair and let it fall to its full length.

9   Now, there were two possessions of the James Dillingham Youngs in which they both took a mighty pride. One was Jim's gold watch that had been his father's and his grandfather's. The other was Della's hair. Had the Queen of Sheba lived in the flat across the airshaft Della would

have let her hair hang out the window some day to dry and mocked at
Her Majesty's jewels and gifts. Had King Solomon been the janitor, with
all his treasures piled up in the basement, Jim would have pulled out his
watch every time he passed, just to see him pluck at his beard from envy.

10   So now Della's beautiful hair fell about her, rippling and shining
like a cascade of brown waters. It reached below her knee and made
itself almost a garment for her. And then she did it up again nervously
and quickly. Once she faltered for a minute and stood still while a tear
or two splashed on the worn red carpet.

11   On went her old brown jacket; on went her old brown hat. With
a whirl of skirts and with the brilliant sparkle still in her eyes, she
fluttered out the door and down the stairs to the street.

12   Where she stopped the sign read: "Mme. Sofronie. Hair Goods of All
Kinds." One flight up Della ran, and collected herself, panting, before
Madame, large, too white, chilly and hardly looking the "Sofronie."

13   "Will you buy my hair?" asked Della.

14   "I buy hair," said Madame. "Take yer hat off and let's have a sight
at the looks of it."

15   Down rippled the brown cascade.

16   "Twenty dollars," said Madame, lifting the mass with a practised
hand.

17   "Give it to me quick," said Della.

18   Oh, and the next two hours tripped by on rosy wings. Forget the
hashed metaphor. She was ransacking the stores for Jim's present.

19   She found it at last. It surely had been made for Jim and no one
else. There was none other like it in any of the stores, and she had
turned all of them inside out. It was a platinum fob chain simple and
chaste in design, properly proclaiming its value by substance alone and
not by meretricious ornamentation—as all good things should do. It
was even worthy of The Watch. As soon as she saw it she knew that it
must be Jim's. It was like him. Quietness and value—the description
applied to both. Twenty-one dollars they took from her for it, and she
hurried home with the 87 cents. With that chain on his watch Jim
might be properly anxious about the time in any company. Grand as
the watch was, he sometimes looked at it on the sly on account of the
old leather strap that he used in place of a chain.

20   When Della reached home her intoxication gave way a little to
prudence and reason. She got out her curling irons and lighted the gas
and went to work repairing the ravages made by generosity added to love.
Which is always a tremendous task, dear friends—a mammoth task.

21   Within forty minutes her head was covered with tiny, close-lying
curls that made her look wonderfully like a truant schoolboy. She
looked at her reflection in the mirror long, carefully and critically.

22   "If Jim doesn't kill me," she said to herself, "before he takes a second look at me, he'll say I look like a Coney Island chorus girl. But what could I do—oh, what could I do with a dollar and eighty-seven cents!"

23   At 7 o'clock the coffee was made and the frying pan was on the back of the stove hot and ready to cook the chops.

24   Jim was never late. Della doubled the fob chain in her hand and sat on the corner of the table near the door that he always entered. Then she heard his step on the stair away down on the first flight, and she turned white for just a moment. She had a habit of saying little silent prayers about the simplest everyday things, and now she whispered: "Please, God, make him think I am still pretty."

25   The door opened and Jim stepped in and closed it. He looked thin and very serious. Poor fellow, he was only twenty-two—and to be burdened with a family! He needed a new overcoat and he was without gloves.

26   Jim stopped inside the door, as immovable as a setter at the scent of quail. His eyes were fixed upon Della, and there was an expression in them that she could not read, and it terrified her. It was not anger, nor surprise, nor disapproval, nor horror, nor any of the sentiments that she had been prepared for. He simply stared at her fixedly with that peculiar expression on his face.

27   Della wriggled off the table and went for him.

28   "Jim, darling," she cried, "don't look at me that way. I had my hair cut off and sold it because I couldn't have lived through Christmas without giving you a present. It'll grow again—you won't mind, will you? I just had to do it. My hair grows awfully fast. Say 'Merry Christmas!' Jim, and let's be happy. You don't know what a nice—what a beautiful, nice gift I've got for you."

29   "You've cut off your hair?" asked Jim, laboriously, as if he had not arrived at that patent fact yet even after the hardest mental labor.

30   "Cut it off and sold it," said Della. "Don't you like me just as well, anyhow? I'm me without my hair, ain't I?"

31   Jim looked about the room curiously.

32   "You say your hair is gone?" he said, with an air almost of idiocy.

33   "You needn't look for it," said Della. "It's sold, I tell you—sold and gone too. It's Christmas Eve, boy. Be good to me, for it went for you. Maybe the hairs of my head were numbered," she went on with a sudden serious sweetness, "but nobody could ever count my love for you. Shall I put the chops on, Jim?"

34   Out of his trance Jim seemed to quickly wake. He enfolded his Della. For ten seconds let us regard with discreet scrutiny some inconsequential object in the other direction. Eight dollars a week or a million a year—what is the difference? A mathematician or a wit would give you the wrong answer. The magi brought valuable gifts,

but that was not among them. This dark assertion will be illuminated later on.

35   Jim drew a package from his overcoat pocket and threw it upon the table.

36   "Don't make any mistake, Dell," he said, "about me. I don't think there's anything in the way of a haircut or a shave or a shampoo that could make me like my girl any less. But if you'll unwrap that package you may see why you had me going awhile at first."

37   White fingers and nimble tore at the string and paper. And then an ecstatic scream of joy; and then, alas! a quick feminine change to hysterical tears and wails, necessitating the immediate employment of all the comforting powers of the lord of the flat.

38   For there lay The Combs—the set of combs, side and back, that Della had worshipped for long in a Broadway window. Beautiful combs, pure tortoise shell, with jewelled rims—just the shade to wear in the beautiful vanished hair. They were expensive combs, she knew, and her heart had simply craved and yearned over them without the least hope of possession. And now, they were hers, but the tresses that should have adorned the coveted adornments were gone.

39   But she hugged them to her bosom, and at length she was able to look up with dim eyes and a smile and say: "My hair grows so fast, Jim!"

40   And then Della leaped up like a little singed cat and cried, "Oh, oh!"

41   Jim had not yet seen his beautiful present. She held it out to him eagerly upon her open palm. The dull, precious metal seemed to flash with a reflection of her bright and ardent spirit.

42   "Isn't it a dandy, Jim? I hunted all over town to find it. You'll have to look at the time a hundred times a day now. Give me your watch. I want to see how it looks on it."

43   Instead of obeying, Jim tumbled down on the couch and put his hands under the back of his head and smiled.

44   "Dell," said he, "let's put our Christmas presents away and keep 'em a while. They're too nice to use just at present. I sold the watch to get the money to buy your combs. And now suppose you put the chops on."

45   The magi, as you know, were wise men—wonderfully wise men— who brought gifts to the Babe in the manger. They invented the art of giving Christmas gifts. Being wise, their gifts were no doubt wise ones, possibly bearing the privilege of exchange in case of duplication. And here I have lamely related to you the uneventful chronicle of two foolish children in a flat who most unwisely sacrificed for each other the greatest treasures of their house. But in a last word to the wise of these days let it be said that of all who give gifts these two were of the wisest. Of all who give and receive gifts, such as they are the wisest. Everywhere they are the wisest. They are the magi.

Gifts of the Magi

JOURNAL

1. **MLA Works Cited** *Using this model, record this story here.*

   Author's Last Name, First Name. "Title of the Story." *Title of the Book.*

   2nd ed. Ed. First Name Last Name. City: Publisher, year. Page number(s) of

   this story. Print.

2. **Main Character(s)** *Describe each main character, and explain why you think each is a main character.*

3. **Supporting Characters** *Describe each supporting character, and explain why you think each is a supporting character.*

4. **Setting and Props** *Describe the setting(s) and all relevant prop(s).*

5. **Sequence**   *Outline the events of the story in order.*

6. **Plot**   *Tell the story in no more than two sentences.*

7. **Conflicts**   *Identify and explain all the conflicts involved here.*

8. **Significant Quotations**   *Explain the importance of each of these quotations. Record the page number in the parentheses.*

   a. "Tomorrow would be Christmas Day, and she had only $1.87 with which to buy Jim a present" (   ).

   b. "One was Jim's gold watch that had been his father's and his grandfather's. The other was Della's hair" (   ).

c. " 'Will you buy my hair?' asked Della" (   ).

d. "For there lay The Combs—the set of combs, side and back, that Della had worshipped for long in a Broadway window" (   ).

e. " 'Dell,' he said, 'let's put our Christmas presents away and keep 'em for a while' " (   ).

9. **Literary Elements**   *Look at this chapter's title and explain why you think this story is placed in this chapter. Explain in which other chapter(s) you might place this story, as relevant to the literary element(s) of that chapter.*

10. **Foreshadowing, Irony, and/or Symbolism**   *Explain examples of foreshadowing, irony, and/or symbolism in this story.*

Follow-up Questions

10 Short Questions

What is the <u>best</u> answer for each?

____ 1. This story is set in
   a. Boston.
   b. Dallas.
   c. New York.

____ 2. The Youngs are
   a. rich.
   b. poor.
   c. middle class.

____ 3. Della's most prized possession is her
   a. apartment.
   b. hair.
   c. watch.

____ 4. Jim's most prized possession
   is his
   a. apartment.
   b. hair.
   c. watch.

____ 5. Della wants to
   a. sell her hair.
   b. pawn Jim's watch.
   c. purchase the combs.

____ 6. Della wants to
   a. buy the combs.
   b. buy Jim's watch.
   c. buy Jim a fob chain.

____ 7. Jim wants to
   a. sell Della's hair.
   b. sell his watch.
   c. purchase the fob chain.

____ 8. Jim wants to
   a. buy the combs.
   b. buy the watch.
   c. buy the fob chain.

____ 9. The gifts are for
   a. Della's birthday.
   b. Jim's birthday.
   c. Christmas.

____ 10. Their celebration
   a. is ruined because of the
      gifts.
   b. is not ruined because of
      the gifts.
   c. is ruined by their losses.

5 Significant Quotations

What is the importance of each of these quotations?

1. "One dollar and eighty-seven cents. That was all."

2. "Now, there were two possessions of the James Dillingham Youngs in which they both took a mighty pride."

3. "'I buy hair,' said Madame."

4. "And now, they were hers, but the tresses that should have adorned the coveted adornments were gone."

5. "'Dell,' he said, 'let's put our Christmas presents away and keep 'em a while.'"

2 COMPREHENSION ESSAY QUESTIONS

Use specific details and information from the story to answer these questions as completely as possible.

1. What are the ironies in this story? Use specific details and information from the story.

2. "Magi" has come to imply "wise men." What is ironic about this title? Use specific details and information from the story.

DISCUSSION QUESTIONS

Be prepared to discuss these questions in class.

1. Do you feel more disappointed for Della or for Jim? Why?

2. Do you think they communicate and understand each other too well or too poorly? Use specific details from the story to explain your thinking.

WRITING

Use each of these ideas for writing an essay.

1. Tell the story of a purchase that you or someone you know worked or saved long and hard for and that turned out not to be worth the effort.

2. Tell the story of an ironic twist in your life or in the life of someone you know.

Further Writing

1. "Gifts of the Magi" is a classic story by O. Henry. Compare the irony in this story to the irony centered on an object in Guy de Maupassant's "The Necklace" (available in a library).

2. Compare the irony of these gifts with the irony of the inheritance in Dorothy Parker's "The Wonderful Old Gentleman" (available in a library).

NOTES

APPENDIX

How *I* Use This Book

This section is *not* intended to tell anyone how to use this book, but rather it is intended to offer insight into some of the many options and possibilities in this book. I am often asked to demonstrate the comprehensive pedagogical apparatus surrounding each story and, since I cannot come out and meet with all of you, this section is an attempt to present at least one instructor's—my!—approach to this book. I truly hope, hope, hope that you use this book as you see fit. The following are simply strategies I use and are offered in response to the many enthusiastic questions I receive.

As has been continually noted, I designed this book most carefully to maximize student learning and teacher efficiency simultaneously. Every entry, every exercise, every word has been most carefully weighed. Following this list, I will explain each entry. However, to streamline this whole section, here are my steps for each story, in a nutshell:

1. First, I do the Sample Lesson with the class, step-by-step, assigning the students to complete the incomplete exercises on their own. I then review, discuss, and/or have students tear out the completed exercises so that I can assess their first journey into this book.

2. Second, with students now ready to start the actual stories, I assign the chapter introduction and the first story in each chapter, then second, and so forth. I introduce any given story via the biographical blurb. Because the blurbs are purposefully written at a more sophisticated level to initiate students into collegiate reading, encourage students to look up words, and so forth, these blurbs are a good place to start discussion. I then assign all vocabulary exercises, pre-reading exercises, and journal exercises, either individually or in groups, depending on the story and the class. Students are to pre-define, pre-think, read, and then reflect upon each story.

3. Third, after each story the students complete, I have students tear out selected pages (one page from vocabulary and one from the Journal selected at random, so that the text is protected and students have to do all the work, because they never know what I will want them to pull out) and I collect the above exercises. By collecting these exercises,

I gain insight into each student's progress and proficiency, I gain necessary and consistent diagnostic and assessment instruments, and I gain students who are well prepared, because they know they will be responsible for their work.

4. Fourth, with exercises collected, I quiz and collect the 10 Short Questions. Although seemingly simplistic, these short questions offer a very efficient measure of each student's comprehension. With students' baseline exercises and comprehension testing collected, I then discuss the story and the correct and/or acceptable answers, as well as relevant test-taking strategies, with the students. These exercises are designed for efficient assessment, so that I am then easily able to numerically grade and return all assignments by the next class.

5. Fifth, depending on the story and the class, I then assign the 5 Significant Quotations, the Comprehension Essay Questions, and/or the Discussion Questions to be completed individually, in groups, or through class-wide discussion. These are intended to be highly flexible and to be used at your discretion.

6. Sixth, for writing classes I then continue to discuss and assign the relevant writing prompts. (Writing is intended for developmental students, while Further Writing is intended for more advanced composition courses.)

7. Seventh, as the semester progresses and some students truly start to excel, I follow the same procedures above but now may do so on an individualized basis, assigning the more demanding stories at the back of the book individually to the more capable students.

There it is briefly. By the time the students have completed each story, they have applied, hands-on, an entire complex of cognitive skills and I have multiple diagnostic and assessment tools. You, of course, should use this book any way you see fit and I hope the above list is merely a concise summary of how I use it. Should you care to read further, here are some more insights I most humbly offer.

In general, I believe that we often learn by doing and that many of our students are capable learners who simply have learned and/or adopted many counterproductive habits. Initiate and then reinforce productive habits by hands-on application and reapplication, and students prosper. To this end, the apparatus surrounding each story is consistent. Students rather rapidly learn appropriate ways to approach stories and, because the apparatus is not only consistent but also most carefully designed to maximize learning, students are learning, prospering, and forming new and more productive habits that will improve all their reading skills and endeavors. Further, among the now several thousand students who have field-tested this book, using this book has dramatically increased performance for both reading and writing students.

Concerning **vocabulary** specifically, the very simple axiom applies that if one cannot understand the words, one cannot read. Reading is a split-second, reception-retrieval-synthesis process. Not knowing words interrupts and thereby breaks down the process. To demonstrate this, try reading this:

> Guardare the chaînon with pithecanthropus, the discovery of zinjanthropus semble démarquer a significato gradino in poursuite.

Now, we are all well-versed, well-read, and hopefully learned, yet unless one is familiar with French, Italian, and some basic cultural anthropology concepts, this is relatively unfathomable, albeit unreadable. Yet this is exactly what collegiate reading material looks like to many of our entering students—every few words have no meaning and the sum total becomes unreadable.

For this reason, each story starts with words in **Context** that are not necessarily the hardest words in the story, but rather that are the most necessary to understanding the story. Thus, in addition to applying context solution skills, each context section also presents the students with the words they will need to know to approach the story, and does so before the students read. While I do not know if each student does the vocabulary before or after each reading, I do know that those who do a poor job or who do not do these exercises at all invariably have problems understanding the given story. These exercises, therefore, simultaneously reinforce context-solving skills for each student while providing you with insight into each student's proficiencies.

Similarly, the **Structural Attack** words apply attack skills for the students and also provide you with insight into each student's proficiencies. These words are chosen because they best apply structural attack skills but, unlike the words in context, these words are not necessarily essential for understanding the story. These exercises also encourage students to use the Glossary and/or a dictionary, therein applying referencing skills.

Concerning **Pre-reading Questions**, these questions are intended to be simplistic and to set the students up for reading efficiently. After using this consistent and tactile model, in time students learn to frame their own pre-reading questions.

Concerning each **biographical blurb**, I often use the blurb to introduce the story. As noted, each blurb is purposefully written at a sophisticated level to link students to collegiate vocabulary and concepts. Because of this, the blurbs often need explanation. Further, each blurb is intended to provide the students with background before reading and referrals for further readings.

Concerning the **Journal**, what can I say? This, to me, is the engine of this book. Here students record, outline, summarize, reflect upon, make sense out of, and even apply MLA documentation format to every story. This is a strenuous and tactile cognitive workout for students as they apply multiple skills, processes, and dynamics to complete it. I always collect the Journal and it is very easy for me to note those students who are having trouble; the Journal clearly demonstrates student acuity, effort, and insight.

Concerning the **Follow-up Exercises**, I quiz and collect the **10 Short Questions** while I collect the vocabulary and journal exercises and before I discuss the story. I give a few minutes in class for those who have already done the questions at home to review their answers and for those who have not done the questions to complete them. While we might assume that students would all do the work beforehand, I am regularly surprised not so much by those who do the questions ahead, as I am by those who do not. I collect this section before discussion for a very simple reason: diagnostically, I need to know what each student has gotten out of the story on her or his own and without my information and/or prompting. These seemingly simplistic questions often demonstrate real confusion and offer invaluable insight into increasing and/or static student proficiencies.

With Pre-reading and Journal exercises and 10 Short Questions collected (which are, again, designed most carefully to be efficient measurement tools and which I will, therefore, easily be able to return by the next class), I now thoroughly discuss the story—and relevant test-taking strategies—with students. I also now turn to the other sections. Depending on the story and/or the class, I may assign the **5 Significant Quotations** and/or the **Comprehension Essay Questions**, or I may use them for discussion. I may assign the **Discussion Questions**, or I may use them for discussion. As noted above, this is a totally fluid area that I designed for your individual discretion. I may choose to use these for discussion in a reading class, and I may choose to assign them for writing in a writing class, or vice versa. These are truly intended to offer you many options.

Finally, the **Writing** prompts speak for themselves. Many of you have commented on how much you like them and there are, again, many options here. I have been privileged to initiate and to chair our learning community program from its very inception. In this program, I teach the same students both reading and writing curricula, and the writing prompts are a natural extension of every story. As noted above, with the now several thousand students who have field-tested this book, we have seen dramatic improvements in both reading and writing students' performances. In fact, many writing instructors are now using this book as the base text in writing courses.

So there it is. This book is designed to meet many, many student needs and to offer a great variety of teaching options. I hope, no matter what ways you choose to use this book, that your students prosper and that you enjoy the book.

Yvonne Collioud Sisko

Glossary of Prefixes and Suffixes

Some words in the **Pre-reading Vocabulary—Structural Attack** are simple words that have been combined or have extra syllables, which make these words look strange or difficult. When you take these words apart, they are usually quite simple to define.

When two or more words are combined to form a new word, the new word is called a **compound word**. By combining the meaning of each of the words, you can define the new word. Look at the word *everyday*. Here, two simple words—*every* and *day*—combine to mean "all the time." Look at the word *worn-whiskered*. *Worn* means "tired" or "old," and *whiskered* implies "old man" or "mature man." Thus, *worn-whiskered* is a word used to describe an old man.

Another way to build a new word is to add a prefix or suffix to a **root** word, or a core word. A **prefix** is a syllable added to the front of the root word that often changes the meaning of the word. A **suffix** is a syllable added to the end of the root word that may alter the use or the meaning of the word. Prefixes and suffixes are called **affixes**. As you define the words in the Pre-reading Vocabulary—Structural Attack exercises, look for and define the root word, and then define the affixes added onto the root word.

For instance, look at the word *provider*. *Provide* is the root word and is a verb that means "to supply." The suffix *-er* at the end means "one who." Thus, the verb *provide* becomes a noun, and the noun *provider* means "a person who supplies something." Now, look at the word *nonprovider*. The prefix *non-* at the beginning means "not" and greatly changes the meaning of the word. *Nonprovider* means "a person who does *not* supply something."

To define the words in Pre-reading Vocabulary—Structural Attack, you need to know the prefixes and suffixes that are listed in Tables G-1 and G-2. Prefixes are defined and are listed in alphabetical order. Suffixes are arranged alphabetically in definition groups. Use the lists to help you in defining these words.

Prefixes

A **prefix** is added to the beginning of a root word. A prefix usually changes the meaning of the root word. *Be especially aware of prefixes because they can greatly change the meaning of a word.* Note that some prefixes have more than one meaning and these meanings may be different.

TABLE G-1
Prefixes

Prefix	Meaning	Application
a-	full of	*Acrawl* means "creeping or spreading everywhere." The town was *acrawl* with gossip when people learned the mayor was arrested.
a-	total absence	*Amoral* means "totally unable to tell right from wrong." When a shark kills, it is *amoral* because a shark does not know right from wrong.
ante-	before	*Antecedent* means "that which comes before." An unkind act may be the *antecedent* to a quarrel.
anti-	against	*Antifreeze* means "a substance that works against or prevents freezing." Vernie uses *antifreeze* in her car during the winter.
be-	full of	*Beloved* means "very much loved." The soldier dearly missed his *beloved* wife.
counter-	against	*Counterplot* means "a plan to work against another plan." The police developed a *counterplot* to ruin the criminals' robbery plan.
de-	against, wrong	*Deform* means "to form badly or wrongly." The fire *deformed* the house and left it twisted and falling down.
de-	out of	*Deplane* means "to get off the airplane." The team claimed their luggage after they *deplaned*.
dis-	not, against	*Distrust* means "not to trust." Allison felt *distrust* toward the salesman who lied to her.
en-	within, into	*Encircle* means "to place in the middle" or "to surround." The floodwaters *encircled* the house.
il-	not	*Illegal* means "not legal." Many laws state that stealing is *illegal* and will place you in jail.
il-	more so	*Illuminate* means "to light up brightly." The fireworks *illuminated* the night sky so brightly that it looked like daylight.
im-	not	*Immeasurable* means "not able to be measured." The joy Teddy felt when he won the championship was *immeasurable*.
im-	more so	*Impoverished* means "very poor." The *impoverished* family did not even have enough money for food.
in-	not	*Incurable* means "not able to be healed." Doug caught an *incurable* disease, which he will have for the rest of his life.

Prefix	Meaning	Application
in-	in, into	*Inside* means "in the side" or "through the side." Michelle walked through the door to get *inside* the room.
inter-	between, among	*Intercollegiate* means "between two or more colleges." Michigan defeated Alabama in *intercollegiate* football.
intra-	within	*Intracollegiate* means "within one college." The red shirts played the blue shirts in the *intracollegiate* gym class competition.
kin-	relative	*Kinfolk* means "the people you are related to or your family." All my *kinfolk* will gather together at Thanksgiving for a family reunion.
non-	not	*Nonaccompanied* means "no company or alone." Bill preferred to attend the party alone, *nonaccompanied* by others.
pre-	before	*Predictable* means "able to be told beforehand." Tom's speeding ticket was *predictable* because he always drives too fast.
re-	again	*Refamiliarize* means "become familiar with again." To pass the test, Jen will *refamiliarize* herself with her notes.
self-	alone, one's own	*Self-satisfied* means "satisfied with oneself." After passing the test, Robert felt good about himself and was quite *self-satisfied*.
semi-	half	*Semiconscious* means "only half or partly aware." With all the noise at the concert, Jake was only *semiconscious* of the sirens outside.
sub-	under	*Subway* means "a road that goes underground." When there is too much traffic on the city roads, it is easier to take the *subway*.
super-	larger, above	*Superman* means "a man larger or better than other men." Bravely running into a burning building to help others is the act of a *superman*.
un-	not	*Unperceived* means "not noticed." Geri usually notices everything, but this time the dirty room went *unperceived*.
under-	below	*Underbrush* means "low shrubs and bushes that grow under the trees." Tony decided to cut the *underbrush* that was growing under his shade trees.
trans-	across	*Transoceanic* means "across the ocean." Alex will catch a *transoceanic* flight from New York to Paris.

Suffixes

A **suffix** is added to the end of a root word. A suffix may have very little effect on the meaning of a word, but a suffix will often change the part of speech of a root word.

What is the part of speech of a word? The **part of speech** of a word is, very simply, the function or use of the word. For instance, look at the word *ski*. In the sentence "Laura's *ski* was damaged," *ski* is a noun—the thing Laura had that was damaged. In "Laura and Ted *ski* downhill," *ski* is a verb—the action Laura and Ted do. In "Laura took *ski* lessons," *ski* is an adjective that describes the kind of lessons that Laura took. The word *ski* remains the same three letters, but the function it serves and the information it communicates change slightly depending on the part of speech it demonstrates. Note that although the use changes—from thing to action to description—the basic idea of a downhill sport remains the same.

In the same way, a suffix may often change the part of speech of a root word while leaving the root word's basic meaning largely unchanged. For instance, if we add *-ed* to the noun and say, "Ted *skied* down the hill," the noun becomes a verb, and the action is in the past. Thus, Ted is still involved with skiing, but now he has done it in the past.

In Table G-2, suffixes you will need to know are listed alphabetically within definition groups and with the relevant parts of speech noted. You will see several words from Pre-Reading Vocabulary—Structural Attack.

TABLE G-2
Suffixes

Suffix	Application
The following suffixes mean "one who" or "that which." Each turns a root word into a noun because the root word becomes the person or the thing that does something.	
-ant	A *servant* is "one who serves." The *servants* cleaned the mansion before the guests arrived.
-ary	A *visionary* is "one who sees clearly or into the future." Einstein was a *visionary* and saw the future uses of nuclear energy.
-ee	A *payee* is "one to whom things are paid." When Dodee owed her brother money, she wrote a check to him and made him the *payee.*
-ent	A *student* is "one who studies." College *students* are usually serious about their studies and work for good grades.
-er	A *fancier* is "one who fancies or likes something." Reid is a proven cat *fancier* and currently has four cats that he loves living in his home.
-ess	A *princess* is "a female who acts like a prince." The *princess* sat on the throne next to her husband, the prince.

Suffix	Application
-folk	*Townsfolk* are "people of the town." The *townsfolk* held a general meeting so that they could all welcome the new mayor.
-ian	A *musician* is "one who plays music." Renée hired several *musicians* so that people would be able to dance at her party.
-ist	A *futurist* is "one who predicts the future on the basis of current trends." *Futurists* advise those in the government in Washington about issues on which it may someday need to enact laws.
-man	A *horseman* is "a person who is skilled at riding and driving horses." Dave is a fine *horseman* who often rides his horse around the park.
-or	A *survivor* is "one who survives or lasts." Rich lasted the longest on the deserted island and was named the *survivor*.

The following suffixes make a root word an adjective, and each changes the meaning of the root word.

-able	*Distinguishable* means "able to be told apart or distinguished." The greasy spots made the dirty clothes *distinguishable* from the clean clothes.
-er	*Lovelier* means, by comparison, "more lovely than another." Missy's garden, filled with blooms, is *lovelier* than Margaret's weed patch.
-est	*Kindliest* means, by comparison, "the most kindly of all." The mother's gentle pat was the *kindliest* touch of all.
-ful	*Frightful* means "full of fright or awful." With all its costumes and noisy bell-ringing, Halloween is a *frightful* night.
-less	*Hapless* means "without happiness or luck" or "unfortunate." The *hapless* student had two flat tires and got a headache on his way to school.
-most	*Uppermost* means "most high" or "important." With a record of no accidents for two years, safety is the company's *uppermost* concern.
-ous	*Nervous* means "full of nerves" or "tense." Kirk was so *nervous* before his test that his hands were shaking.

The following suffixes mean "related to," "like," or "having the quality of" and generally change the meaning of a root word very little. Mostly, they change the parts of speech of the root word.

-al	The noun *cone* means "a form that comes to a circular point" and becomes the adjective *conical*. The tip of the space shuttle is rounded and *conical*.
-ance	The verb *repent* means "to feel sorry about" and becomes the noun *repentance*. After he broke his Mom's favorite vase, John felt awful and was filled with *repentance*.
-ant	The verb *observe* means "to see" and becomes the adjective *observant*. Carrie watches everything closely and is very *observant*.

Suffix	Application
-ed	The noun *candy* means "something sweet" and becomes the adjective *candied*. Mom used lots of sugar to sweetly coat the *candied* apples.
-ed	The noun *ink* means "writing fluid" and becomes the past-tense verb *inked*. Jefferson took pen and *inked* his signature on the Declaration of Independence that he wrote.
-en	The verb *choose* means "select" and becomes the adjective *chosen*. He had joined the Marines and became one of the *chosen* few.
-ence	The verb *depend* means "to rely on" and becomes the noun *dependence*. When Lisa paid her own bills, she knew her *dependence* on her parents would end.
-ic	The noun *metal* means "shiny element" and becomes the adjective *metallic*. Laura's silvery dress had a *metallic* shine.
-ing	The verb *terrify* means "to scare" and becomes the adjective *terrifying*. The *terrifying* thunder scared all of us as it seemed to shake the whole house.
-ish	The noun *fever* means "internal heat" and becomes the adjective *feverish*. Joel felt *feverish* from the heat of his sunburn.
-ism	The adjective *ideal* means "perfect" and becomes the noun *idealism*, which means "belief in perfection." George's *idealism* often leaves him disappointed because things are not always perfect.
-ity	The adjective *stupid* means "unthinking" and becomes the noun *stupidity*. Alice could not believe her *stupidity* when she locked her keys in the car.
-ive	The noun *feast* means "cheerful meal" and becomes the adjective *festive*. The wedding, with all its foods and colorful flowers, was a most *festive* affair.
-ly, ily	The adjective *stealthy* means "moving quietly" and becomes the adverb *stealthily*. Bob crept so *stealthily* in the backdoor that no one knew he had entered the house.
-ment	The verb *confine* means "to restrain" and becomes the noun *confinement*. When the children misbehaved, Dad sent them to their rooms for silent *confinement*.
-ness	The adjective *nervous* means "tense" and becomes the noun *nervousness*. It was very hard for the groom to overcome his *nervousness* on his wedding day.
-tation	The adjective *ornamental* means "decorated" and becomes the noun *ornamentation*. Her diamond rings and pearl necklaces created *ornamentation* fit for a queen.
-ty	The adjective *frail* means "delicate" and becomes the noun *frailty*. At Aunt Alice's ninetieth birthday, we were all concerned about her *frailty*.
-y	The noun *stone* means "hard item" and becomes the adjective *stony*. The policeman had a *stony* look when the boy who was driving did not have a license.

Credits

Chapter 1: *Page 28:* "Salvation" from THE BIG SEA by Langston Hughes. Copyright © 1940 Langston Hughes. Copyright renewed 1968 by Arna Bontemps and George Houston Bass. Reprinted by permission of Hill and Wang, a division of Farrar, Strauss and Giroux, LLC. *Page 39:* "Eleven" From WOMAN HOLLERING CREEK. Copyright © 1991 by Sandra Cisneros. Published by Vintage Books, a division of Random House Inc.. And originally in hardcover by Random House Inc. By permission of Susan Bergholz Literary Services, New York, NY and Lamy, NM. All rights reserved. By permission of Susan Bergholz Literary Services, New York, NY and Lamy, NM. All rights reserved. *Page 50:* "The Kiss" by Kate Chopin.

Chapter 2: *Page 64:* "The Hockey Sweater" from The Hockey Sweater and Other Stories copyright © 1979 by House of Anansi Press. Reprinted with permission. *Page 75:* "Trail of the Green Blazer" from MALGUDI DAYS by R.K. Narayan, copyright © 1972, 1975, 1978, 1980, 1981, 1982 by R.K. Narayan. Used by permission of Viking Penguin, a division of Penguin Group (USA) Inc. *Page 87:* "Strong Temptations—Strategic Movements—The Innocents Beguiled" by Mark Twain.

Chapter 3: *Page 101:* "Bone Girl" by Joseph Bruchac © 1993 in EARTH SONG, SKY SPIRIT. *Page 116:* "Wine on the Desert". Copyright © renewed 1968 by the Estate of Fredrick Fraust. *Page 132:* "The Tell-Tale Heart" by Edgar Allan Poe.

Chapter 4: *Page 147:* "Ah Bah's Money" by Catherine Lim. *Page 159:* "The Story of an Hour" by Kate Chopin. *Page 170:* "Gifts of the Magi" by O. Henry.

Index

Note: The **bolded** locators refers to stories in the text.